The Methodist Primer

METHODIST EVANGELISTIC MATERIALS

1908 Grand Avenue
Nashville 5, Tennessee

World Methodism Today

	Membership	*Community*
EUROPE		
British Isles	800,800	2,368,500
Continental Europe	145,200	251,800
AMERICA		
United States of America	14,312,815	29,347,350
Canada	1,017,000	2,596,000
Mexico	27,550	47,500
Central & South America	82,900	177,700
Atlantic & Caribbean Islands	95,700	241,800
AFRICA		
South Africa	703,000	2,250,000
Nigeria	84,200	135,200
Other Countries	298,300	611,300
ASIA		
India	735,900	1,913,000
Japan	179,000	310,000
Philippine Islands	140,500	221,500
Other Countries	176,420	535,900
AUSTRALASIA		
Australia	350,000	1,000,000
Other Islands	123,500	451,000
GRAND TOTAL	**19,272,785**	**42,458,550**

These figures are taken from the *Handbook of Information* issued by the World Methodist Council. They are all inclusive, and represent the total of all Methodist bodies in the countries concerned. The figures for Canada represent the proportionate share of Methodists who went into the United Church of Canada, while those for Japan are for the Church of Christ in Japan, into which the Japanese Methodist Church merged in 1940. While some of the figures are estimates (especially in the second column), they are based on the best factual information that it was possible to gather.

Twenty-eighth Printing
Revised
Total printed: 1,250,000

Printed in the United States of America

CONTENTS

PREFACE

"The average Methodist needs and desires a concise account of the story of his Church. This book is an attempt to supply in simple language and in brief form certain information on the history, doctrines, organization, and activities of The Methodist Church. . . .

"I send forth this modest volume in the hope that it will be one factor in the making of a more intelligent and loyal membership."

Thus wrote Bishop Charles C. Selecman in launching THE METHODIST PRIMER.

This is the same PRIMER that was produced by the fertile mind and the warm heart of Bishop Charles C. Selecman, revised slightly and brought up to date each year.

It is untouched in its original form and design. That which is changed from time to time is what is affected by the legislation of the General Conference, whatever changes there might be in the "Fields of Service," especially overseas, and whatever changes are made necessary in statistical figures and reports. In fact, such changes were already being made each year by the editor during the lifetime of Bishop Selecman, at Bishop Selecman's request.

Many times Bishop Selecman made the remark that, during the ages, he might become known not so much as having been a pastor, or the president of a great university, or even as a Methodist bishop, as having been the author of THE METHODIST PRIMER. So might it be. THE METHODIST PRIMER is his imperishable monument.

GEORGE H. JONES, *Editor*

THE LIFE OF MR. WESLEY

By Dr. Coke and Mr. Moore

"Respecting such a man, even the smallest particulars will not be unpleasing. He was, in his person, rather below the middle size, but remarkably well proportioned. He had what some call a clean constitution in a high degree. He seemed not to have an atom of superfluous flesh, and yet was muscular and strong. His whole person was expressive of the activity and health, which generally arises from strong bodily powers, preserved by temperance and exercise. His face was remarkably fine, even to old age. The freshness of his complexion continued to the last week of his life. His whole countenance was highly expressive and interesting: it has often been observed that many who were deeply prejudiced against him have been changed in a moment into sentiments of veneration and esteem, on being introduced into his presence.

"He was a pattern of neatness and simplicity, not only in his person, but in every circumstance of his life. In his chamber and study, during his winter months of residence in London, we believe there never was a book misplaced, or even a scrap of paper left unheeded. He could enjoy every convenience of life; and yet, he acted in the smallest things, like a man who was not to continue an hour in one place. He seemed always at home, settled, satisfied and happy: and yet was ready every hour to take a journey of a thousand miles.

"His conversation was always pleasing, and frequently interesting and instructive in the highest degree. By reading, traveling, and continual observation, he had a fund of knowledge, which he dispensed with a propriety and perspicuity, that we believe has been rarely equalled. The Greek and Latin classics were as familiar to him as the most common English authors; and so were many of the best French writers. Yet, though so richly furnished, we believe those of the most improved taste have never observed in him the affectation of learning. He joined in every kind of discourse that was innocent. As he knew that all nature is full of God, he became all things to all men in conversing on these subjects."

CHAPTER I

HISTORY

Thomas Carlyle describes the Eighteenth Century in the brief caustic phrase "Soul extinct, stomach well alive."

John Wesley was born in the third year of this century. "According to the grace of God, as a wise masterbuilder," he laid the foundation of THE METHODIST CHURCH on the Word of God.

In the beginning there was no plan to organize a new Church. The eighteenth-century revival of religion which swept over England among the common people, inspired and led by John and Charles Wesley and their associates, and the course of events that followed that great revival, made the organization of a new Church necessary. The result was THE METHODIST CHURCH, which reaches around the world.

THE WESLEY FAMILY

In order to understand THE METHODIST CHURCH, its origin, its spirit, its doctrines, and its organization, it is important to know something of the Wesley family.

The Reverend Samuel Wesley, father of John and Charles Wesley, was the son of John Wesley and the grandson of Bartholomew Westley, all three of whom were graduates of Oxford and clergymen in the Church of England. He was rector of the church at Epworth, a small village about one hundred miles north of London. He married Susanna Annesley, daughter of Dr. Samuel Annesley, an English clergyman. She was the youngest of twenty-five children. He had a struggle meeting the needs of his large family on a small salary. He was a man of high principle, deep piety, and strict conscience. While his sons were in college, he wrote them letters full of religious advice.

Susanna Wesley

Susanna Annesley at an early age, and of her own choice, was confirmed in the Established Church of England. Her father, recognizing her rare talents, gave her the best education available at the time. Her strong, independent mind led her to differ with her preacher-father and later to many differences of opinion with her husband. However, her married life was a fruitful and happy one.

She was the mother of nineteen children. She was by nature a teacher. She had little respect for the common methods of instructing and governing children. Therefore she taught her children at home. "She made education a wonderful adventure." Each child was expected to master the alphabet on the fifth anniversary of its birthday. Then followed a careful course of training. She also set apart an hour each week for each child for prayer and religious instruction. Thursday evening after dinner was little Jackie's (John Wesley's) hour. This made a deep impression on him. Later in life when he was away from home he wrote asking his mother still to keep that hour for him. She was a gifted writer of letters to her sons when they were away in college. She gladly consented for John and Charles to take the long, perilous journey to America as missionaries, saying, "Had I twenty sons I should rejoice were they all so employed, though I never saw them more."

For some time after her husband's death she lived about with her children. At the age of seventy she went to London and thereafter made her home with John. At the ripe age of seventy-eight, she lay dying in the parish house of Wesley Chapel, City Road. She rallied to say to her children who were about her bed-side:

"Children, when I am released, sing a psalm of praise."

By all tests Susanna Wesley must have been one of the world's most wonderful women.

In Samuel and Susanna Wesley we have a rare combination

of noble ancestry, native ability, acquired culture, economic sagacity, strict discipline, human sympathy, moral goodness, religious fervor, and common sense. Their home was the cradle of THE METHODIST CHURCH. Out of the Epworth rectory, or parsonage home, came three celebrated scholars and preachers, Samuel, John, and Charles.

John Wesley

John Wesley was born in Epworth, England, June 17, 1703. He died in London, March 2, 1791, in his eighty-eighth year. The first ten years of his life were spent in the Epworth parsonage. From ten until seventeen he was a pupil in Charterhouse School in London. When seventeen, he entered Christ Church College, Oxford University, on a scholarship of £40, (or about $160.00). Five years later he graduated from Oxford. He was ordained Deacon September 19, 1725, elected a fellow of Lincoln College, Oxford, 1726, and awarded the degree of Master of Arts in 1727. He was ordained a Priest in the Church of England, September 22, 1728.

He did not decide upon his life work until after his graduation from Oxford. But when he made his choice he gave himself to his work with such industry and prayerfulness that he is a wonder to all who study his travels and labors. As a fellow at Oxford he wrote that famous phrase, "Leisure and I have taken leave of each other." For more than fifty years he preached an average of three times a day, a total of 42,400 sermons. He often rode on horseback from sixty to seventy miles a day, covering in his land journeys 250,000 miles. When he was seventy-five years of age he speaks of having traveled 280 miles in forty-eight hours.

He published 440 books, tracts, and pamphlets.

At Oxford he developed his daily plan of study, which was: Mondays and Tuesdays, Greek and Latin; Wednesdays, logic and ethics; Thursdays, Hebrew and Arabic; Fridays, Metaphysics and Natural Philosophy; Saturdays, Oratory and Poetry; Sunday, Divinity.

9

Charles Wesley

Charles Wesley, the eighteenth child, was five years younger than his brother, John. Charles declined adoption by a rich uncle and was elected to Christ Church College, Oxford, in 1726. He was ordained in 1735.

Charles Wesley was an eloquent preacher, and preceded John in field preaching. He is best known, however, by his hymns. It was in singing the hymns of Charles Wesley and repeating parts of them to one another that the early Methodists kept alive the flame of divine fire that was in their hearts. By these hymns the people became acquainted with Methodist doctrines. At the heart of his great hymns are the vital Christian doctrines—the atonement, love, grace, assurance, eternal life, mercy, pardon, praise, and adoration. He wrote 6,500 hymns, 56 of which are in our present *Methodist Hymnal*. Chief among his hymns in popularity is "Jesus, Lover of My Soul." Other noted hymns of Charles Wesley are: "Love Divine, All Loves Excelling"; "A Charge to Keep I Have"; "O, for a Thousand Tongues to Sing"; "Hark, the Herald Angels Sing."

He was the "poet laureate of the Methodist movement." Charles shared with John the labors, the hardships, the persecutions, the joys, and the triumphs of the eighteenth-century revival.

The First Methodist Society

John Wesley wrote the following account of the first society called Methodist:

"In November, 1729, four young gentlemen of Oxford —Mr. John Wesley, Fellow of Lincoln College; Mr. Charles Wesley, Student of Christ Church; Mr. Morgan, Commoner of Christ Church; and Mr. Kirkman, of Merton College—began to spend some evenings in a week together, in reading chiefly the Greek Testament. The next year, two or three of Mr. Wesley's pupils desired the liberty of meeting with them; and afterwards one of Mr. Charles Wesley's pupils. It was in 1732 that Mr.

Ingham, of Queen's College, and Mr. Broughton, of Exeter, were added to their number. To these, in April, was joined Mr. Clayton, of Brazen-nose, with two or three of his pupils. About the same time Mr. James Hervey was permitted to meet with them, and afterwards Mr. Whitefield."

This club was started by Charles Wesley during the second year of his student life at Oxford (1727). He persuaded two or three others to join with him in organizing a society. They met first every Sunday evening, then two evenings a week, and finally every evening from six until nine o'clock. Their meetings and deportment attracted the attention of both faculty and students.

John Wesley was not at Oxford when the society was first formed. When he returned, he immediately associated himself with the society and was recognized as its head. Their activities included the study of the Bible in Hebrew and Greek; the study of the classics; visits to the prison and the poor and sick; and religious instruction of poor children. At the time the work of the society was so novel that the news of it spread beyond Oxford. They met with both praise and harsh criticism. The society was called by various names, such as Bible Moths, The Reformers' Club, The Godly Club, The Enthusiasts, and The Holy Club. One of the students said, "Here is a new sect of Methodists sprung up." The name Methodist stuck. Though it was sometimes applied in derision, the Wesleys welcomed the term. Today millions of people in all parts of the world are happy to bear the name Methodist.

The Mission to America

When General James Oglethrope was organizing his colony for Georgia, he desired that some clergymen go to minister to the spiritual needs of the colonists and as missionaries to the Indians. John Wesley volunteered and Charles was chosen as secretary to General Oglethrope. They sailed from Gravesend,

October 21, 1735, on board the ship "Simmonds," with about 80 other English and 26 Moravians, including women and children.

On this voyage, John Wesley was much impressed by the Moravians. They were a very pious group, with a strong and simple faith in God. They were calm when the storms rocked the small ship. Fear was absent, faith in God dominant. A new kind of Christian experience was opening to him.

In Georgia he was kindly received by most of the people, and worked diligently at his task. He preached and administered the sacraments of the Church of England in English, German, French, Italian, and Spanish. He organized a society of the more studious and serious, patterned after the Oxford society.

After his return to England, John referred to that society as the first Methodist Society after Oxford. He had great expectations for his work with the Indians. He thought he would find them with open minds, "as little children willing to learn and eager to do the will of God." To use his own words, however, they were "gluttons, thieves, liars and murderers." They were so well content with their manner of living that they would brook no interference by Wesley nor permit him to come among them. The leaders told Wesley that they were too busily engaged with wars to hear him. All of Wesley's advisers, including Oglethorpe, insisted that the time had not yet come to establish a Christian mission among the Indians. He was greatly disappointed, for he considered the mission to the Indians his chief duty to America.

Trouble arose for Wesley in Savannah. He was so strict in his church discipline and so plain in his preaching to the colonists that many were offended and turned against him. He patiently bore these wrongs for a while, but seeing that his mission to the Indians could not be fulfilled and having never engaged permanently to care for the Church of England in Georgia, he decided to return to England. He sailed from America, December 22, 1737, a discouraged man.

In his journal is this entry:
> "I shook off the dust off my feet, and left Georgia, after having preached the gospel there (not as I ought but as I was able) one year and nearly nine months."

As he sailed back to England meditating over his Georgia experiences, he wrote in his journal:

> "I who went to America to convert the Indians have never myself been converted to God."

Later he wrote on the margin, "I doubt this."

It is true, however, that he left a real consciousness of God in the hearts of many Indians, and the little Methodist Society he organized in Georgia may rightly be called the forerunner of THE METHODIST CHURCH in America.

A few years later, Whitefield, coming to Georgia, wrote:
> "The good John Wesley has done in America is inexpressible. His name is very precious among the people, and he has laid a foundation that I hope neither man nor devils will ever be able to shake."

Wesley's Heart-Warming Experience

John arrived in London February 3, 1738, after an absence of two years and nearly four months. He was restless. Doubt and fear surged in his heart like the billows of the sea. He longed for the peace and calm assurance of his Moravian friends. He talked often with Peter Bohler, one of the Moravian leaders in London. These conversations led him to a new understanding of saving faith and to the opening of the chapter in his life which we know as his *heart-warming experience*. Wesley carefully records his experience as follows:

"WEDNESDAY, MAY 24, 1738

"I think it was about five this morning, that I opened my Testament on those words, 'There are given unto us

13

exceeding great and precious promises, even that ye should be partakers of the Divine nature,' 2 Pet. 1:4. Just as I went out, I opened it again on those words, 'Thou art not far from the kingdom of God!' In the afternoon I was asked to go to St. Paul's.

"The anthem was:

> 'Out of the deep have I called unto thee,
> O Lord: Lord, hear my voice.
> O let thine ears consider well
> The voice of my complaint.
> If thou, Lord, wilt be extreme
> To mark what is done amiss,
> O Lord, who may abide it?
> For there is mercy with thee;
> Therefore shalt thou be feared.
> O Israel, trust in the Lord;
> For with the Lord there is mercy,
> And with him is plenteous redemption.
> And he shall redeem Israel from all his sins.'

"In the evening I went very unwillingly to a society in Aldersgate Street, where one was reading Luther's *Preface to the Epistle to the Romans*. About a quarter before nine, while he was describing the change which God works in the heart through faith in Christ, I felt my heart strangely warmed. I felt I did trust in Christ, Christ alone for salvation; and an assurance was given me, that he had taken away my sins, even mine, and saved me from the law of sin and death."

This was a turning point in Wesley's life. After this experience he was full of joy, and faith, and courage. He still had times of trial and burden, but he became a different man, if we may judge by his labors and his great success.

Now begins the great, fruitful epoch in Wesley's life. It cannot be traced solely to what happened at Aldersgate. His home training, his education, his self-discipline, his industry, his wonderful personality, and ability must not be forgotten. As I have said elsewhere on this matter, "You can not set fire to a vacuum." An undisciplined, untrained man after Aldersgate would have been unable to be the leader of a great spiritual movement. But all these, without his experience of assurance, were not sufficient.

Wesley's preaching was not such as to please the rectors of the Church of England. His doctrines differed from theirs. His language seemed too plain. His zeal and fire were offensive to them. Church after church was closed to him. At Oxford when he returned to preach, he was criticized and never invited back. In 1739 the rector in a church in London preached a sermon in which he attacked "certain modern enthusiasts" and advised his followers to "shun them as you would a deep plague." The Bishop of Bristol said to him, "You have no business here; you are not commissioned to preach in this diocese. Therefore I advise you to go hence." But Wesley's answer to the Lord Bishop was "The world is my parish."

Returning to his father's former church at Epworth, he found himself locked out by the rector. He stood on his father's tombstone in the church yard and spoke to the assembled throng on the text:

"The Kingdom of God is not meat and drink; but righteousness, and peace, and joy in the Holy Ghost."

This in a way portrays his future ministry, which was largely to be outside of the Church for the masses.

"A thousand locked church doors became for him only a thousand reasons why he should go into the open fields and, finally, into the whole world."

Charles Wesley was blessed with the heart-warming experience three days before John. He too was driven from pulpits and persecuted but he calmly faced danger in declaring the truth. The preaching and singing of the Wesleys started the great religious revival so sorely needed in England in the Eighteenth Century.

George Whitefield

One morning at Oxford, Charles Wesley invited George Whitefield to breakfast. George was a poor boy working his way through college. The breakfast visit led George to join the Methodist group. Whitefield was the first of the group to begin field preaching, and on his insistence John Wesley first preached in the open. Whitefield's career in England and America is an unbroken record of travels and labors as a flaming evangelist.

On his numerous visits to America, he ranged from Georgia to New England, preaching Christ. He died on this side of the Atlantic and is buried in Newburyport, Massachusetts. As one evidence of the profound influence he had in America, his statue stands on the campus of the University of Pennsylvania as a founder of that famous institution.

The United Society

The revival spread. The opposition and persecution served only to intensify the zeal of the Methodists and to spread the news of their work throughout England. Naturally the followers of Wesley, having received new faith and joy and hope, would come together to exchange their experiences and talk of their new relation to God. This gave rise to the organization of Methodist societies in London, Bristol, and other towns and villages. Methodist chapels were also built. The cornerstone of the first Methodist chapel was laid in Bristol, May 12, 1739.

Wesley was a genius in organization. He proposed to form these societies into a United Society. His well-known account of the formation of the United Society is as follows:

"In the latter end of the year 1739 eight or ten persons who appeared to be deeply convicted of sin, and earnestly groaning for redemption, came to Mr. Wesley in London. They desired, as did two or three more the next day, that

16

JOHN WESLEY

THE CONSECRATION OF FRANCIS ASBURY

AN EARLY GENERAL CONFERENCE

FRANCIS ASBURY
Pioneer American Bishop

he would spend some time with them in prayer, and advise them how to flee from the wrath to come, which they saw continually hanging over their heads. That he might have more time for this great work, he appointed a day when they all might come together; which from thenceforward they did every week, namely on Thursday, in the evening. To these, and as many more as desired to join with them (for their number increased daily), he gave advices from time to time which he judged most needful for them; and they always concluded their meetings with prayer suited to their several necessities.

"This was the rise of the United Society, first in Europe, and then in America. Such a society is no other than a company of men having the form and seeking the power of godliness, united in order to pray together, to receive the word of exhortation, and to watch over one another in love, that they may help each other to work out their salvation."

The General Rules

There was only one condition previously required of those who desired membership in the Society, viz.:

"A desire to flee from the wrath to come, and be saved from their sins."

But those who desired to continue in the Society were expected to evidence their desire for salvation:

First: by doing no harm, avoiding evil of every kind, especially that which is most generally practiced; such as, taking the name of God in vain, profaning the day of the Lord, drunkenness, buying or selling spirituous liquors, fighting, quarreling, brother going to law with brother, breaking the Golden Rule, softness, making bad debts, borrowing or buying without the probability of paying.

Second: by doing good of every possible sort and, as far as possible, to all men.

17

Third: by attending upon all the ordinances of God.
(See Methodist *Discipline* for the General Rules.)

These simple General Rules signify the high moral standards set for early Methodists. The Methodist movement was more than a wave of religious enthusiasm. It demanded a pure motive, a joyful experience, and a blameless life.

They were not required to accept or affirm a creed. To this day conduct rather than creed is the test of membership in THE METHODIST CHURCH.

The preaching and singing of this gospel of REPENTANCE, JUSTIFICATION by FAITH, NEW LIFE in CHRIST JESUS, and the WITNESS of the SPIRIT gradually overcame opposition and gained wide acceptation. The revival swept over England, Scotland, Wales, Ireland, and on to America. In ever-increasing breadth and depth, the sermons and labors of John Wesley and the hymns of Charles Wesley were heralded throughout the land.

The First Yearly Conference

The rapid increase of the Methodist societies required more preachers and a closer organization. Wesley chose lay preachers and set them apart to do the full work of the ministry, except the administration of the sacraments.

On June 25, 1744, Wesley called a few preachers together for a *conference.* They met in the Foundry Church, London. The conference consisted of six clergymen of the Church of England and four lay preachers. From that time until his death Wesley held a conference every year. The conference consisted of questions asked by Wesley and for the most part answered by him. Wesley appointed the preachers to their several fields of labor and changed them at will. This yearly conference was a step toward Church organization. The conferences of 1745, 1746, and 1747 gave serious consideration to Church government, polity, and history.

Question of the Sacraments

Very few of the preachers in connection with Mr. Wesley were ordained. Therefore, they could not administer the sacraments. The people called Methodists were urged to accept Baptism and the Holy Communion at the hands of the rectors of the Established Church. But most of the Methodists were not members of the Church of England and could not, for this reason, be admitted to the sacraments even if they had so desired. Therefore, a widespread demand arose for the ordination of Methodist preachers.

Wesley appealed to the Bishop of London to ordain at least one of the Methodist preachers so that others might be ordained and the Methodist movement conserved in the Church of England. But the Bishop of London refused. Very early Wesley realized that the demand for an ordained ministry was just. He carefully weighed the question and finally brought about the ordination of Richard Whatcoat and Thomas Vasey. Because of his love and devotion to his own Church, only an urgent necessity and a divine duty as a last resort seemed to justify such an act on his part.

Methodism in America

As in England, so in America, John Wesley laid the foundation for THE METHODIST CHURCH. The day before Wesley arrived home from Georgia, George Whitefield sailed for America, neither knowing the plans of the other.

In 1760 Phillip Embury and Robert Strawbridge, local Methodist preachers, came to America from Ireland. Embury organized the first Methodist Society in New York in 1766. Strawbridge organized the first Methodist Society in Maryland, probably sometime during the year 1763.

Among the British troops in New York at this time was Captain Thomas Webb. He had been converted under Wesley's preaching and joined a Methodist Society in England in 1765 and immediately set apart as a lay preacher. He assisted Embury in building the first Methodist Meeting House in New York

19

which was dedicated October 30, 1768. He was instrumental also in planting Methodist Societies in Long Island, New Jersey, Pennsylvania, and Delaware.

Captain Webb and others appealed to Wesley to send preachers to America. Wesley presented this appeal to the Leeds Conference in 1769. Richard Boardman and Joseph Pilmoor volunteered and were sent by Wesley to America. They began their work October 21, 1769.

As the work in America grew, the second call for help was sent to Wesley. Richard Wright and Francis Asbury were sent. They reached Philadelphia October 27, 1771. Asbury soon became the leading force in American Methodism and was appointed by Wesley as assistant superintendent for America.

None of these preachers was ordained with the probable exception of Strawbridge. He probably had been ordained by a German minister. At any rate he administered the sacraments and the people gladly received them at his hands. Asbury and the other preachers, following the example of Wesley, insisted that the Methodists receive the sacraments at the hands of the clergy of the Church of England.

After the Revolutionary War, however, the colonists were entirely separated from England, nearly all the English clergymen having returned to England. Therefore, the Methodists were without preachers to whom they could look for the sacraments. Both laymen and preachers appealed to Wesley. It was unmistakably clear to Wesley that the urgent necessity and the divine imperative for ordaining Methodist preachers was at hand.

Therefore, after calm deliberation, on September 1, 1784, assisted by Thomas Coke and James Creighton, also Presbyter of the Church of England, he ordained Richard Whatcoat and Thomas Vasey deacons. The next day he ordained them elders. Then, assisted by Creighton, Whatcoat, and Vasey, he ordained Thomas Coke superintendent.

Coke, Whatcoat, and Vasey immediately prepared to sail for America to fulfill their important mission. They landed in New

York November 3, 1784. Dr. Coke revealed his mission to John Dickins, the Methodist preacher in New York, who cordially approved the plan and told Dr. Coke that all preachers in America would approve it.

Coke then proceeded to Barratt's "Chapel in the Woods" in Delaware, where he preached Sunday, November 14. Francis Asbury and a few preachers he had called for consultation were in the service. In the afternoon, Coke and Asbury held a private conference, and went over the whole plan. Asbury expressed doubt, but when they laid the matter before the other preachers they were unanimous for it.

Asbury insisted, however, that all of the preachers should be consulted on a matter of so grave importance. They therefore agreed to call a conference of all the preachers in Baltimore, on the twenty-fourth day of December, 1784. On the day appointed about sixty of the preachers met at Lovely Lane Chapel, Baltimore. Most of the preachers were single men under thirty years of age. This is known as the Christmas Conference. Several things were done:

1. Francis Asbury and Thomas Coke were elected superintendents.
2. By adopting a resolution offered by John Dickins, a Church was formally organized and named Methodist Episcopal Church.
3. Francis Asbury was ordained deacon on Saturday. On Sunday he was ordained elder, and on Monday was consecrated or ordained superintendent.
4. The Articles of Religion and the Sunday service prepared by John Wesley for Methodists in North America were adopted.
5. On motion of John Dickins the conference voted its approval for the establishment of a school. It was afterwards known as Cokesbury College (after Coke and Asbury).
6. Twelve other preachers were elected and ordained elders.
7. A program of expansion was outlined.

Thus during the Christmas Season, 1784, the first Methodist

Church in America, and in the world, began its historic mission.

After a session of ten days the preachers departed for their widely separated fields, following the wagon trails of the early settlers. The Methodist Circuit Rider began his epoch-making career as evangelist, pastor, organizer, and builder. Often he was also the schoolmaster and founder of schools and colleges. Usually a single man living on a salary of "$64.00 and no more" per year, he traveled on horseback with his scant supply of clothing and books in saddle pockets. He preached in homes, mostly of the log-cabin type, at camp meetings, and in rude chapels. There were only 83 traveling preachers and less than 15,000 members in 1784. By the time of Asbury's death (in 1816) there were 200,000 members and more than 700 ordained preachers. Such a multiplication of disciples has seldom been known in the history of the Church, since the marvelous expansion in the first centuries of the Christian era. In this way the Lord of the harvest set His seal upon His faithful ministers. In the ardent language of their time, they were "given souls for their hire." Most of them succumbed to the hardships of the wilderness, to exposure, fever, and other maladies and went early to their graves. But they faltered not. "God buries His workmen but carries on His work" was the maxim oft upon their lips. They followed the trail of the pioneers, the woodman's axe, the farmer's plow, and on this virgin soil they scattered the seed of gospel truth, the harvest of which is our heritage today, THE METH-ODIST CHURCH, ten million strong.

Francis Asbury

Francis Asbury is known as "The Prophet of the Long Road." It was aptly said that "he printed the map of his ministry with his horse's hoofs." For travels he even surpassed John Wesley, and that in an undeveloped country. "Asbury outrode Wesley. All in all it has been estimated that he covered 275,000 miles. He crossed and recrossed the Allegheny Mountains more than sixty times." From his Journal it has been gleaned that "he went into New York State more than 50 times; New Jersey over 60;

Pennsylvania, 78; Maryland, 80; North Carolina, 63; South Carolina, 46; Virginia, 84; Tennessee and Georgia, each 20; Massachusetts, 23 times after his first visit there in 1791; and in other States and Territories with corresponding frequency." He preached 16,000 sermons, an average of one a day for half a century.

Once he said, "My brethren seem not to know the way to the country, and I think I shall show them the way." On and on he rode, in feeble health, in "pain, pain, pain," as he once wrote in his journal. He rode until age and infirmity made it necessary for him to have a traveling companion. On he rode, preaching mostly to small groups, until within a few days of his death.

When on his way to America, he wrote in his journal, "Whither am I going? To the New World. What to do? To gain honor? No, if I know my own heart. To get money? No; I am going to live to God and to bring others so to do." American Methodism is what it is today largely because of Francis Asbury, the first bishop of the Methodist Episcopal Church.

Growth, Divisions, and Union

After the historic Christmas Conference, the Methodist Episcopal Church in the United States of America had a steady and substantial growth. It extended its boundaries; strengthened its Episcopacy; ordained preachers; began writing a Discipline, setting forth a constitution and body of law to govern the Church; increased the number and functions of the Annual Conferences; divided the Annual Conferences into districts; created the office of Presiding Elder; held revivals and camp meetings from one end of the nation to the other; carried the gospel where it had never been; founded schools and colleges; gathered into its membership people of all races and classes; established missions and built churches all over the nation.

From time to time differences arose that resulted in divisions. The first secession of colored people occurred in 1816, and the African Methodist Episcopal Church was formed. It is now the largest Methodist Church consisting wholly of the Negro race.

23

Methodist Protestant Church

The Methodist Protestant Church was organized in 1830 in Baltimore. A group of godly and pious men were asking for a larger share for laymen in the government of the Church. This being denied at the time, they separated from the Methodist Episcopal Church. Within eight years its membership grew to 50,000. This Church carried on bravely for more than a century, and made a noble record in missions, education, and evangelism. It came to pass that the major bodies of Methodism so modified their rules as to give laymen, including women, the desired recognition. This helped to open the way for union.

M. E. Church, South

In the year 1844, when the nation was driving headlong to the tragic days of the War between North and South, when heated debates stirred the land from border to border over the question of slavery, came "the days of great sorrow in Methodism." In the General Conference of that year, meeting in New York, the storm broke over Bishop James O. Andrew, who is described as a "timid and peaceful bishop." He had just married a wife who owned slaves. He was quite willing to manumit the slaves or to resign, but being the center of such a storm, his friends urged him not to resign. But he was not acceptable in the North so long as he owned slaves. The laws of the Southern States prohibited the freeing of slaves. After days of prayerful and tearful discussion, the Plan of Separation was proposed "to meet the emergency with Christian kindness and strictest equity." The plan was adopted June 7, 1844.

The next year on May 1, 1845, about one hundred delegates duly elected by the Annual Conferences of the Southern States met in Louisville, Kentucky. After a thorough and prayerful consideration of all questions involved, on May 17, 1845, a resolution was adopted by which the Annual Conferences in the slave-holding states were constituted a separate ecclesiastical connection under the Plan of Separation. Thus the Methodist Episcopal Church, South, was organized. As Dr. Harry Woolever

24

says in his pamphlet entitled *The Highroad of Methodism,* "It was not a secessionist Church. It was a sister Church."

Although some disagreements followed over property rights, yet for nearly one hundred years the two sister Churches lived and labored side by side. They were steadily drawn more closely together and for years commissions labored to form a suitable plan of union. Finally a commission composed of representatives of the Methodist Episcopal Church, the Methodist Episcopal Church, South, and the Methodist Protestant Church formulated a plan of union which each of the three Churches adopted.

The Uniting Conference, provided for in the Plan of Union, composed of 900 delegates, met in the great convention hall, in Kansas City, Missouri, on the tenth day of May, A.D. 1939. In the presence of sixty bishops and more than 10,000 visitors, the 900 delegates unanimously adopted the following Declaration of Union:

We, the members of the Uniting Conference, the legal and authorized representatives of the Methodist Episcopal Church, the Methodist Episcopal Church, South, and the Methodist Protestant Church, in session here assembled on this the tenth day of May, 1939, do solemnly in the presence of God and before all the world make and publish the following Declaration of fact and principle:

I

The Methodist Episcopal Church, the Methodist Episcopal Church, South, and the Methodist Protestant Church are and shall be one United Church.

II

The Plan of Union as adopted is and shall be the constitution of this United Church, and of its three constituent bodies.

III

The Methodist Episcopal Church, the Methodist Episcopal Church, South, and the Methodist Protestant Church had their common origin in the organization of the Methodist Episcopal Church in America in 1784, A.D., and have ever held, adhered to and preserved a common belief, spirit, and purpose, as expressed in their common Articles of Religion.

IV

The Methodist Episcopal Church, the Methodist Episcopal Church, South, and the Methodist Protestant Church, in adopting the name 'The Methodist Church' for the United Church, do not and will not surrender any right, interest or title in and to these respective names, which, by long and honored use and association, have become dear to the ministry and membership of the three uniting Churches and have become enshrined in their history and records.

V

The Methodist Church is the ecclesiastical and lawful successor of the three uniting Churches, in and through which the three Churches as one United Church shall continue to live and have their existence, continue their institutions, and hold and enjoy their property, exercise and perform their several trusts under and in accord with the Plan of Union and *Discipline* of the United Church; and such trusts or corporate bodies as exist in the constituent Churches shall be continued as long as legally necessary.

VI

To The Methodist Church thus established we do now solemnly declare our allegiance, and upon all its life and service we do reverently invoke the blessing of Almighty God. Amen.

Thus three major American Methodist communions became THE METHODIST CHURCH with 7,590,411 members, 21,687 effective ministers, and 25,197 pastoral charges. The total value of property was $656,474,867.00, and the total annual budget $80,453,997.00. This represents the growth of one branch of Methodism in a period of two hundred years. In the language of John Wesley, "The best of all is, God is with us."

The World Family of Methodism

While naturally this Primer must deal principally with the section of world Methodism whose members it seeks chiefly to serve, we should always remember the rock from which we were hewn.

True to the genius of her founder, British Methodism has progressed vigorously during her two centuries of service, and today a great united Methodism gives its witness in Great Britain, with an independent Conference in Ireland.

British Methodism, like ourselves, has seen a number of mission Conferences stem out. Today she with her daughter Conferences is a great power in world Methodism.

In the Pacific, Australasian Methodism has a Triennial General Conference covering the work of five State Annual Conferences in Australia and Tasmania. New Zealand and Tonga have independent Conferences, and these share with Australasian Methodism in vigorous mission activities in the Pacific.

In South Africa is another independent Conference, while mission areas on that continent are still linked with Great Britain.

In Ceylon, India, China and elsewhere are active British Methodist missions. With the full concurrence of British Methodism, her missions in South India are joining in the United Church of South India, while in Canada Methodism was a leading group in establishment of the great United Church of Canada.

Since 1881, these British sections have joined with the American Methodist Church and her mission Conferences and kindred bodies, in holding World Conferences of Methodism. The most recent was held at Oslo, Norway, during August, 1961.

Methodism is a world Church with a *world* vision.

MEMBERSHIP OF THE METHODIST CHURCH, LAY AND MINISTERIAL
FOR YEAR 1963

JURISDICTION	PREPARATORY MEMBERS	LAY MEMBERS	MINISTERS
Northeastern	459,071	1,958,545	5,440
Southeastern	233,184	2,802,032	7,560
Central	57,194	371,846	1,481
North Central	593,491	2,338,946	6,354
South Central	268,841	2,021,808	5,442
Western	168,745	713,112	2,420
Totals	1,780,526	10,206,289	28,697

Full Members (Lay and Clerical) 10,234,986
Preparatory Members 1,780,526

Total Full and Preparatory 12,015,512

CHAPTER II

DOCTRINE

"It was not a new doctrine but new life the first Methodists sought for themselves and for others. To realize in the hearts of men the true ideal of Christianity, to maintain its personal experience and to extend it—this was their design; and their system of government grew up out of this and was accordingly shaped by it."

By this we do not assert that John Wesley and his followers placed little emphasis upon Christian truth. On the contrary, two great historic documents stand boldly forth in the literature of early Methodism, the Apostles' Creed and the Twenty-Five Articles of Religion.

The Apostles' Creed

"I believe in God the Father Almighty, Maker of heaven and earth; and in Jesus Christ, His only Son our Lord; who was conceived by the Holy Spirit, born of the Virgin Mary, suffered unto Pontius Pilate, was crucified, dead, and buried; the third day He rose from the dead; He ascended into heaven, and sitteth at the right hand of God the Father Almighty; from thence He shall come to judge the quick and the dead. I believe in the Holy Spirit; the holy catholic Church, the communion of saints; the forgiveness of sins; the resurrection of the body, and the life everlasting. Amen."

This ancient statement of Christian faith has come down from the early Church, probably the second century. As has been aptly said, it is a body of Christian doctrine which, like a stream, flowed from the apostolic fountain. The use of this creed does not separate us from other followers of Christ. It binds us more closely to them.

In brief, the Apostles' Creed affirms faith in:

1. God the Father.
2. Jesus Christ His Only Son.
3. The Holy Spirit.
4. The Church.
5. Forgiveness of Sins.
6. The Resurrection
7. Life Everlasting.

Probably the great majority of the congregations of Methodism repeat this Apostles' Creed every Sunday.

Other Affirmations of Faith

In *The Book of Worship for Church and Home,* authorized by the 1944 General Conference for voluntary and optional use (and available from The Methodist Publishing House), are four other Affirmations of Faith: The Nicene Creed, A Modern Affirmation, The Korean Creed, and A Creed in the Words of St. John. Two of these are included in the Aids to Worship in *The Methodist Hymnal* and are used from time to time by Methodist congregations:

1. A Modern Affirmation

The Minister: Where the Spirit of the Lord is, there is the one true Church, Apostolic and Universal, whose Holy Faith let us now reverently and sincerely declare:

The Minister and People: We believe in God the Father, infinite in wisdom, power and love, whose mercy is over all His works, and whose will is ever directed to His children's good.

We believe in Jesus Christ, Son of God and Son of man, the gift of the Father's unfailing grace, the ground of our hope and the promise of our deliverance from sin and death.

We believe in the Holy Spirit as the Divine Presence in our lives, whereby we are kept in perpetual remembrance of the truth of Christ, and find strength and help in time of need.

We believe that this faith should manifest itself in the service of love as set forth in the example of our blessed Lord, to the end that the kingdom of God may come upon the earth. Amen.

2. The Korean Creed

We believe in the one God, Maker and Ruler of all things, Father of all men; the source of all goodness and beauty, all truth and love.

We believe in Jesus Christ, God manifest in the flesh, our Teacher, Example, and Redeemer, the Saviour of the world.

We believe in the Holy Spirit, God present with us for guidance, for comfort and for strength.

We believe in the forgiveness of sins, in the life of love and prayer, and in grace equal to every need.

We believe in the Word of God contained in the Old and New Testaments as the sufficient rule both of faith and of practice.

We believe in the Church as the fellowship for worship and for service of all who are united to the living Lord.

We believe in the kingdom of God as the divine rule in human society; and in the brotherhood of man under the Fatherhood of God.

We believe in the final triumph of righteousness and in life everlasting. Amen.

Articles of Religion *

The Articles of Religion were sent to America by John Wesley, who simply selected those articles of the Church of England which he deemed best suited to the Church in the New World. He selected only twenty-four of the thirty-nine articles. One article, No. 23, applies to our national government. More than half of these are a protest against the errors of Roman Catholicism. "Our Methodist Articles are protestant articles."

The substance of the twenty-five articles may be stated briefly as follows:

1. There is one true God, who has all power, wisdom and goodness. He made and preserves all things. Father, Son and Holy Spirit are one God, the Trinity.

---

* See Methodist *Discipline* (pages 30-37) for Articles of Religion.

31

2. Jesus the divine Son of God was born of the Virgin Mary, was crucified, dead and buried for the sins of men.

3. Jesus Christ rose from the dead and ascended into heaven. He will return at the last day to judge all men.

4. The Holy Spirit came from the Father and the Son and is one with them in the Trinity.

5. The Holy Scriptures (or the Bible) contain all truth necessary for salvation.

6. The ancient rites and ceremonies of the Old Testament do not bind Christians. But its moral teachings should be obeyed.

7. Original sin is the evil in man's nature which he inherits.

8. The free will of man must have divine help in order that he may do good and please God.

9. We are justified, or pardoned, not by good works, but by faith in our Lord and Saviour Jesus Christ.

10. Good works are the fruits of faith and are pleasing to God.

11. It is not possible to do more good works than God requires.

12. If one sins after justification, or pardon, he may repent and be forgiven.

13. The Church of Christ is a congregation of faithful men in which the gospel is preached and the sacraments are administered.

14. Purgatory is not taught in the Bible; neither is praying to saints or worshiping images or relics.

15. Public worship should not be conducted in a language which the people do not understand. To do so is contrary to the Word of God and the custom of the early Christian Church.

16. Sacraments are badges of Christian profession and signs of God's grace. Christ ordained only two sacraments: Baptism and the Supper of the Lord.

17. Baptism is a sign of Christian profession. The baptism of young children should be retained in the Church.

18. The Sacrament of the Lord's Supper is a sign of brotherly love and also a memorial of Christ's death. It should be observed in a spiritual manner, but should not be made an object of worship.

19. In the Lord's Supper lay members should receive both bread and wine.

20. There is no value in masses for the dead. This is a dangerous deceit.

21. Ministers may marry at their own discretion.

22. It is not necessary to have the same rites and ceremonies in all places. These may be changed to meet the needs of different countries and times.

23. This article states the authority and independence of our national government.

24. Christians may possess private property, but they should give liberally to the poor.

25. A Christian may swear, when a magistrate requires it, without violating the teachings of the Bible.

The Twenty-Five Articles of Religion were formally adopted by the famous Christmas Conference of 1784 which organized the Methodist Episcopal Church in America. Since then, they have been given a prominent place in the *Discipline*. But they are not to be regarded as a Methodist product.

Prominent Doctrines of Methodism

Although THE METHODIST CHURCH is not committed to a distinct body of doctrine, peculiar to itself, it has emphasized certain great truths of Christian experience that have come to be known as our heritage "Roman Catholicism is a doctrine of the Church, Calvinism a doctrine of God, Methodism a doctrine of religion." We mention here the following prominent doctrines of THE METHODIST CHURCH:

1. God is infinite in wisdom, power, and love. His boundless love and tender mercy are for the whole world. Charles Wesley wrote in one of his great hymns, "Thy nature and thy name is love." Therefore, "Whosoever will" may come. (See John 3:16.)

2. Jesus Christ came to show forth God's love for the world. He died for all men. No one was left out.

3. All have sinned and fallen short of the glory of God and

33

therefore need a divine Saviour who can say "Thy sins which are many are all forgiven."

4. Those who truly repent and believe on the Lord Jesus Christ are born again. This is called the **new birth, regeneration** or **conversion.** To quote Bishop McConnell, "In Methodist thought today, as in the beginning, everything turns around the resolution to follow Christ. Methodist belief is that the surrender leads to transformation to life. One can phrase the theory of how this is done to suit oneself, but one cannot abandon the idea of passage into new life through surrender to the Divine will without abandoning something essentially Methodistic." . . .

5. The Spirit bears witness to those who are born again that they are children of God and joint heirs with Jesus Christ. **The Witness of the Spirit** may be said to be the distinguishing doctrine of Methodism. This belief is not peculiar to Methodism, however, nor to any other Church. John Wesley, in his great sermon on the subject, says: "By the witness of the Spirit I mean the inward impression on the soul, whereby the Spirit of God immediately and directly witnesses to my spirit that I am a child of God; that Jesus Christ hath loved me and given Himself for me; that all my sins are blotted out, and I, even I, am reconciled to God."

This joyous experience of personal salvation was also expressed in Charles Wesley's hymns; for example:

> My God is reconciled,
> His pardoning voice I hear;
> He owns me for His child,
> I can no longer fear.

6. **A life of joy and obedience** should follow repentance and the new birth. "If any man be in Christ, he is a new creature; old things have passed away; behold all things are become new."

7. **Sanctification** is another cardinal doctrine of Methodism. John Wesley described it as a life fully surrendered to love God with the whole heart and our neighbors as ourselves. This experience is sometimes called "perfect love."

Paragraph 86 of the *Discipline* reads as follows:

"Sanctification is that renewal of our fallen nature by the Holy Ghost, received through faith in Jesus Christ, whose blood of atonement cleanseth from all sin; whereby we are not only delivered from the guilt of sin, but are washed from its pollution, saved from its power, and are enabled, through grace, to love God with all our hearts and to walk in his holy commandments blameless.

8. **Childhood religion** has been stressed by THE METHODIST CHURCH from the beginning. John Wesley was truly a pioneer in the religious instruction of children. His memory of his own early religious training under his mother doubtless had much to do with his great interest in childhood religion. In fact, it has been ably argued that he preceded Robert Raikes in establishing Sunday Schools. From the first the Methodists practiced infant baptism. (See Articles of Religion, XVII.) It has also approved of the reception of children, when properly instructed, into the membership of the Church and has provided a special Order for Receiving Children and Youth into the Church. (Paragraph 1915, *Discipline*.) Many of the great leaders of Methodism have gladly testified that they professed their love for Christ and became members of the Church at the early age of 6, 7 or 8, and have never known a time when they did not desire to love and endeavor to serve God. The conclusive answer to those who question the wisdom of this practice is, "By their fruits ye shall know them." The divine Master who said, "Suffer the little children to come unto me, and forbid them not, for of such is the kingdom of God," has set His seal upon childhood religion.

9. **Christian experience.** THE METHODIST CHURCH has emphasized the personal element in religion. Christianity is a matter of "heart and life." Without laying down any pattern of experience in repentance, faith, conversion or assurance, Methodism has proclaimed that a life of joy and peace should flow from fellowship with Christ and His people. It is not too much to say that our theology and our ecclesiastical system are the product or outgrowth of a vital Christian experience.

10. **Catholicity.** Bishop Mouzon defined *the holy Church* as "A Church broad enough to embrace all who worship and serve Jesus Christ, and preaching a gospel large enough to meet all the spiritual needs of all men." That represents the broad spirit of Methodism. John Wesley said, "I desire a league offensive and defensive with every follower of Jesus Christ." To quote Dr. Gilbert T. Rowe: "Finally, as among Protestants, Methodism stands for an inclusive Christianity. It believes that the things that unite Christians are far more important than the things that divide. It has no exclusive doctrines, rites or ceremonies." It teaches that all men are included in the atonement and the gospel invitation; that all must repent and believe on the Lord Jesus Christ; that all followers of Christ may have access to the sacraments of baptism and the Lord's Supper; and that ordination by any established evangelical Church is valid. A letter from any Christian Church may be accepted as the only condition of membership. Moreover, it has been our historic custom to cooperate with other Churches in evangelism, missions, education, reform, social service, and the promotion of various movements for the extension of the Kingdom. This has brought THE METHODIST CHURCH into active relationships with the American Bible Society, The National Council of Churches, The World Council of Churches, The World Conferences on Faith and Order, Life and Work, Missions, and numerous other interdenominational bodies. Furthermore, this spirit and practice is carried down to the local church. Any follower of Christ is invited to commune with us. Any minister in good standing may be invited to our pulpits. We lay no claim to exclusiveness in doctrine, rites or authority. We request only a place of fellowship and service in the ranks of those who love our Lord Jesus Christ in sincerity. In the words of the text of John Wesley's famous sermon on Fraternity: "If thy heart be right with my heart, give me thy hand." THE METHODIST CHURCH recognizes "the Christians of other Churches and the Churches of other Christians."

11. **The Church.** Let no one conclude from the foregoing paragraph that a true Methodist is lacking in intelligent loyalty to his own Church. The great sentence that stands at the

very beginning of the Order for Receiving Persons into the Church expresses our profound conviction: "Dearly Beloved, the Church is of God, and will be preserved to the end of time, for the promotion of His worship and the due administration of His word and ordinances, the maintenance of Christian fellowship and discipline, the edification of believers, and the conversion of the world." This sentence states the divine origin, the permanent nature and the broad mission of the Church. Before one can be recieved into membership in THE METHODIST CHURCH (except by letter or transfer) he is required to take this solemn obligation: "Will you be loyal to THE METHODIST CHURCH, and uphold it by your prayers, your presence, your gifts, and your service?" That is a sweeping promise, and embraces loyalty, prayer, presence, gifts and service. This puts the Church in a place of primary importance in the life of the individual and of society. No true Methodist will speak lightly of his Church or treat it with irreverence or neglect. He will remember that "Christ loved the Church and gave Himself for it." He will fearlessly face the fact that the principles of Jesus will not win their way in the world without the leadership of the Church. From his heart he will sing with reverence and gratitude:

> I love Thy Church, O God!
> Her walls before Thee stand,
> Dear as the apple of Thine eye,
> And graven on Thy hand.

12. As stated above it has been the custom of THE METHODIST CHURCH to cooperate with other churches in various fields of service. It is also true that from the beginning Methodism has proclaimed the necessity of the application of Christianity to every area of life. One evidence of this fact is The Methodist Social Creed. The first paragraph is: "The interest of THE METHODIST CHURCH in social welfare springs from the gospel, and from the labors of John Wesley, who ministered to the physical, intellectual, and social needs of the people to whom he preached the gospel of personal redemption."

This position was affirmed by the Christmas Conference (1784) in the expressed desire to "reform this continent and spread scriptural holiness throughout the land." The same high ground has been re-affirmed by the action of succeeding General Conferences. Our desire is to "seek first the Kingdom of God and His righteousness." Our prayer is, "Thy Kingdom Come. Thy will be done."

13. The Methodist teaching and practice on Christian baptism is clearly stated by Bishop John M. Moore in *Methodism in Belief and Action*. "It is a covenant; it is a commitment to Christ and His Kingdom; it is a rite of initiation into that body of which Christ is the head; it is the symbol of purification; it is the emblem of the baptism by the Spirit of God. . . . . It is the sign and seal of a new spiritual birth."

Believing as Bishop Moore asserts that three modes of baptism—sprinkling, pouring, and immersion—were practiced by the early Church and that all three modes have been practiced ever since, THE METHODIST CHURCH approves and accepts any one of these if performed by an authorized minister or priest.

14. As stated above, THE METHODIST CHURCH also admits to the Sacrament of the Lord's Supper all followers of Christ who desire to partake with us of the symbols of the body and blood of our Lord and Saviour Jesus Christ. The invitation is: "Ye that do truly and earnestly repent of your sins, and are in love and charity with your neighbors, and intend to lead a new life, following the commandments of God, and walking from henceforth in his holy ways; draw near with faith and take this holy Sacrament to your comfort; and, devoutly kneeling, make your humble confession to Almighty God." To quote Bishop Moore again: "The taking of the Sacrament of the Lord's Supper is the supreme act of worship of any Christian. It cannot be neglected or slightly regarded without possible religious peril."

Therefore every Methodist church should observe this sacrament with regularity and all members should attend upon this means of grace.

CHAPTER III

GOVERNMENT

In the foregoing Chapter the statement is made that our form of government grows out of and is shaped by Christian experience. For example, the development of the conference system of Methodism had its humble beginnings in London in June, 1744. John Wesley called together ten preachers, six of whom were clergymen of the Church of England, and four of whom were lay preachers, to consider with him certain questions which he presented. The conference consisted of questions asked by Wesley. After discussion of these questions by the group, the answers were recorded for the most part in the terse, direct language of Mr. Wesley. From this lowly origin in the old Foundry Church, London, there has grown up a simple and workable system of conferences.

Many eminent writers in the field of Church government have spoken in highest praise of John Wesley as an ecclesiastical statesman and of our government as unsurpassed as an effective instrument for the accomplishment of the spiritual mission of the Church.

As the Church has grown in numbers, and interests have multiplied in the fields of evangelism, education, missions, charitable institutions and other worthy causes, the one small conference which was held each year by John Wesley from 1744 until his death has developed into six conferences. To each conference certain duties or functions have been assigned by the *Discipline* of the Church. They are:

1. The General Conference,
   which meets once in four years.
2. The Jurisdictional Conference,
   which meets once in four years.
3. The Annual Conference,
   which meets once a year.

4. The District Conference,
   which meets once a year.
5. The Quarterly Conference,
   which meets four times a year.
6. The Church Conference,
   which meets once a year.

The General Conference

The one law-making body of THE METHODIST CHURCH is The General Conference, which has full power in matters of a general nature. Conditions, privileges and duties of Church Membership are determined by it; also, matters pertaining to ministerial orders, and the powers and duties of Annual, District, Quarterly, and Church Conferences. The General Conference alone can enact laws or rules defining the "powers, duties and privileges of the Episcopacy." Such matters as the Hymnal and Ritual, the judicial system, the publishing interests, evangelism, education, missions, and other benevolent connectional enterprises are decided by it. The General Conference is authorized "to enact such other legislation as may be necessary," subject to five restrictive rules.

The *Restrictive Rules* are part of the Constitution of the Church. They provide:

1. The General Conference shall not revoke or change our Articles of Religion.
2. It shall not "do away Episcopacy or destroy the plan of our itinerant general superintendency."
3. Ministers and members may not be expelled from the Church without a trial.
4. The General Conference shall not revoke or change the General Rules.
5. The produce of the Publishing House is secured to the benefit of "superannuated and worn-out preachers, their wives, widows and children."

Note. For full text of Restrictive Rules see the *Discipline,* ¶ 9, which is Section II of the Constitution.

The General Conference meets once in four years "in the month of April or May." Delegates to this legislative body are elected by the Annual Conferences. One-half of the delegates shall be ministers and one-half lay members. In 1964 the General Conference may be increased to 1,400 delegates.

The Jurisdictional Conference

The Jurisdictional Conference came into being in 1939, as a part of The Plan of Union. Dr. Harry Earl Woolever, author of *The Highroad of Methodism,* says: "The outstanding provision of the Plan of Union is that which calls for six Jurisdictional Conferences in the United States: the Northeastern, Southeastern, North Central, South Central, Western, and Central. The Central includes the organized Negro Conferences and Missions. . . . The Jurisdictional Conferences elect their own Bishops, determine the boundaries of their Annual Conferences and promote the evangelistic, educational, missionary and benevolent programs of the Church." The Plan of Union provides that delegates shall be elected by the Annual Conferences, one-half of whom shall be ministers and one-half lay members. (See Map of Jurisdictional Boundaries, inside front cover.)

The Central Conference

On mission fields the conference which corresponds to the Jurisdictional Conference is called the Central Conference. The Central Conferences have the privilege of electing their own bishops who exercise the functions of their office only within their own territory, but are privileged to participate in all meetings of the Council of Bishops. When Central Conferences elect to do so, they may choose their bishops for a term of years rather than for life.

The Annual Conference

As its name indicates, the Annual Conference meets once a year, at which time Pastors, District Superintendents and other ministers are assigned to their work for the following year.

41

The Annual Conference is composed of ministerial members who are called Traveling Preachers, and Lay Members, one of whom is elected by each Pastoral Charge. Lay Members must be at least twenty-one years of age, and members of a constituent church for the four years preceding their election.

The Annual Conference is the basic body in the Church. Such fundamental matters are referred to it as, 1. Constitutional Amendments. 2. Election of delegates to General and Jurisdictional Conferences. 3. Matters relating to ministerial character and orders.

The Conference also hears reports of boards, committees and institutions and lays plans for the work of the coming year. The bishop in charge presides over the Annual Conference. In his absence the Conference may elect a President.

The reading of the appointments at the close of an Annual Conference is one of the most spectacular events in Methodist procedure. In recent years it is not the occasion of suspense as was the case in the early history of the Church in America. The *Discipline* provides that the bishop or district superintendent shall consult a minister before his appointment is announced at the Annual Conference. (See ¶ 432.) Therefore, arbitrary appointments are rarely necessary. "The Church has advanced from the idea of an autocratic episcopacy to the idea of a bishop as an arbiter of all interests involved. It is a bishop's business in making appointments to hear all parties from which any light can possibly come, and then to make the decision." (McConnell.)

To be sure the bishop's decision may not be altogether satisfactory. For example, several churches may desire a popular minister; or several pastors may look favorably upon the same church. All cannot be pleased. Our system, however, insures a pastor for every charge and a charge for every pastor. Unemployed ministers or charges without pastors are rarely found in THE METHODIST CHURCH. The custom of grouping rural or village churches in one pastoral charge, called a circuit, saves travel and generally provides a resident pastor.

The District Conference

Each Annual Conference may authorize a District Conference in each District, at which the District Superintendent shall preside. The membership and duties of the District Conference are set forth in the *Discipline* in paragraphs 686 to 691. The duties are many and varied, such as: (1) Inquiring into the spiritual state of the church, (2) Missionary and evangelistic work in the districts, (3) Christian education, (4) Woman's work, (5) Support of the church colleges, (6) The American Bible Society, (7) Lay Activities, especially Christian stewardship and serving unoccupied sections, (8) Hospitals and Homes, (9) Church papers and Publishing House, (10) Candidates for the ministry, (11) Candidates for other forms of Christian service, (12) Support of the church, its ministry and benevolences.

The Quarterly Conference

The Quarterly Conference is the basic body of control within a pastoral charge. It unites the charge with connectional Methodism and promotes all plans, policies, and programs of THE METHODIST CHURCH through the local constituency. This gives it a place of great importance in the local church and in the charge, which may consist of more than one church.

The Quarterly Conference is composed of the preachers, lay leaders, stewards, and trustees of the various churches, certain officers and representatives of the church schools and Woman's Societies, and certain others designated by the *Discipline*. The presiding officer is the District Superintendent or an Elder (a minister in Elder's orders) designated by him.

While the Quarterly Conference got its name because it was held *quarterly,* provision is now made whereby only two Quarterly Conferences must be held, the first and the fourth, during the Conference year. The second and the third Quarterly Conferences may be either omitted or held at the discretion of the District Superintendent.

The Quarterly Conference transacts the business committed

43

to it by the *Discipline* and indicated on the Official Quarterly Conference record blanks. To it is committed the general oversight of the Official Board and other duties, such as: to receive reports from the pastor, the church officers, commissions, committees, and societies of the churches of the charge; to elect officers of the church or churches (stewards, trustees, lay leaders, church school superintendents, etc.); to set up the required commissions and desired committees; to determine courses of action; to recommend proper persons for license to preach; to determine the amount to be accepted for the promotion of World Service and Conference benevolences; and to work with the District Superintendent in promoting the total Methodist program and all the spiritual and temporal interests of the church —evangelistic, education, missionary, and benevolent.

Among the committees recommended but not required, the following are suggested: Nominations, Pastoral Relations, Records and History, Co-operation, Policy, Parsonage, Farm and Home, Lay Personnel, Wills and Legacies, Apportionments, and Christian Vocations.

The duties of these committees are briefly stated in the *Discipline*. For example, the Committee on Pastoral Relations shall help supply the pulpit in the absence of the pastor and, by counsel, shall aid the pastor in making his ministry most effective. The committee shall be amenable to the Quarterly Conference, and when a change of pastors is felt desirable for the best interests of the pastor and of the churches, its relation to "the district superintendent and bishop shall be advisory only." For the committee to attempt to select or "call" a pastor would conflict with the duties assigned to the Bishop and District Superintendent and thereby destroy the Methodist itinerancy.

Trustees and Church Property

Another important duty of the Quarterly Conference relates to church property. The Board of Trustees is made "responsible to the Quarterly Conference" in all matters relating to church or parsonage property and any other "real estate and personal property." The Board of Trustees is made responsible to the Quarterly Conference in respect of (1) titles (2) income from property, (3) building funds, (4) debts, (5) insurance, (6) legal papers and (7) investment of any trust funds. It is clearly provided however that the "Trustees shall not prevent or interfere with the Pastor" in the use of the church property for religious services and other proper meetings. Also they shall not "permit the use of said property for religious or other meetings without the consent of the pastor, or in his absence of the District Superintendent." Important provisions are made safeguarding the management, sale, and mortgaging of property. Written "consent of the District Superintendent" must be secured before there is a mortgage or sale. The Quarterly Conference must duly authorize the transaction. Ten days' notice of any meeting for this purpose must be given from the pulpit of the church or churches concerned, including notice of the proposed action. The call for a Quarterly Conference can be made only by the District Superintendent.

The trustees of a church or a charge hold the property in trust for the church or charge, subject to the direction of the Quarterly Conference and to the provisions of the *Discipline*. The trustees must act according to the will of the Quarterly Conference; they have no power to act otherwise and can be removed from office for failure to do so.

The Trust Clause in deeds to churches and parsonages lies at the foundation of our system and is a vital part of our Methodist itinerancy. It provides that church and parsonage property shall be "subject to the *Discipline,* usage and ministerial appointments of said church, as from time to time authorized and declared by the General Conference and by the Annual Conference within whose bounds the said premises are situated. This provision is solely for the benefit of the grantee, and the grantor reserves no right or interest in said premises."

A local church may be incorporated when the Quarterly Conference deems such corporation best for the interests of the church and to conform with the laws of the state, county, or country. When so directed by its Quarterly Conference, the Board of Trustees shall immediately perform all actions for enacting the incorporation. All articles of incorporation, and proposed amendments thereto, must conform to the provisions of the *Discipline,* and must be approved in writing by the District Superintendent (¶¶ 176-178).

The Official Board

Every Methodist church has an "administrative body" called the Official Board, usually spoken of as "the Board." This board is responsible to the Quarterly Conference and reports to it. It is the duty of the pastor and the District Superintendent to see that this board is properly organized and that it functions properly. The pastor, stewards, *ex officio* stewards, and trustees (who are Methodists) are members of this board (see *Discipline,* ¶ 207, ¶ 209).

Great care should be taken to see that only persons of worthy character are members of this board, for in the eyes of the church and of the outside world, the board members represent the church. Therefore, the General Conference has specified that "only morally disciplined persons shall be so nominated, with special reference to total abstinence from alcoholic beverages." It is further specified that stewards "shall be persons of genuine Christian piety who love the church and are competent to administer its affairs."

Ex officio stewards are persons who hold certain high offices and positions of trust in the organizations of the church which entitle them to be stewards and members of the Official Board. They automatically become members of the board just as soon as they assume these offices; and they cease to be members of the board just as soon as they no longer hold the offices. These persons are: (1) the church lay leader; (2) the church business manager, if any, and if a member of the local church; (3) the director of Christian education or the educational assistant; (4-8) the chairman of each of the five commissions: Membership and Evangelism, Education, Missions, Stewardship and

Finance, and Christian Social Concerns; (9) the secretary of stewardship; (10, 11) the lay delegate and his first alternate to the Annual Conference; (12, 13) the presidents of the Woman's Society of Christian Service and Methodist Men; (14) the church treasurer; (15) the financial secretary, if any, and if a member of the local church; and (15, 16) the presidents of the Young Adult Fellowship and of the Methodist Youth Fellowship or Youth Council.

The Board shall meet monthly, both at stated times and upon call, to look after the "spiritual and temporal" affairs of the church. Among the duties of the board, these are significant:

1. To promote and have oversight of the total work of the local church, under the direction of the pastor.

2. To receive the reports of the five commissions, the various committees, and all the organizations of the church.

3. To consult with the pastor and recommend to the Quarterly Conference concerning the salary of the pastor.

4. To inform and educate the congregation concerning the World Service program and conference benevolent causes, and to promote World Service Sunday each month (fourth Sunday) in the church and church school.

5. To promote the program of lay activities, in cooperation with the pastor and lay leader.

6. To arrange for visitation of the entire constituency of the church.

7. Under the pastor, to plan and approve the program and work of the church and to take such action as is deemed best for the well-being and progress of the church.

8. To attend to all responsibilities entrusted to it by the Quarterly Conference and the law of the church.

The Five Commissions

As churches vary in size and interests, so will they vary in organization, in the number of projects they sponsor, and in the size of the programs they promote. Large churches will have many more organizations and committees than will small ones. Small churches may be forced to reduce their organization and program to a minimum. But, according to the *Discipline,* "No local church, however small, is adequately and effectively organized unless there is set up a minimum structure for participating in five of the major concerns of the Church Universal—evangelism, education, missions, stewardship, and Christian social concerns."

No church is organized sufficiently unless it is organized to take care of these concerns in an adequate way. Therefore, every Methodist church *must* have five Commissions, each one of which is specifically entrusted with one of these concerns.

These Commissions are elected by the Quarterly Conference (or the Official Board—see *Discipline,* ¶ 219) and are aids to the Official Board, being its chief administrative agencies. The *Discipline* specifies who shall be on each of these Commissions, and gives each Commission both guidance and instruction in what to do (¶¶ 220-275). There is an official report blank for each of these Commissions.

1. **The Commission on Membership and Evangelism** shall seek out the unsaved and the unchurched and strive to lead them to salvation in Christ and into the fellowship of the church. Moreover, it shall seek out negligent and inactive members and seek to restore them to active participation in the church's life and fellowship. The specific duties listed in the *Discipline* for this Commission include such practical plans and programs as religious surveys, goals for persons to be won, promotion of church attendance, prayer groups, friendly visitation, personal and visitation evangelism, private and family worship, the reading of the Holy Scriptures, and the organizing of new churches (see ¶¶ 222,126). The General Board of Evangelism is the general agency of the church corresponding to this commission in the local church.

2. **The Commission on Education** shall provide for the Christian education of the entire membership and constituency

of the church. It determines the policies of the church school, of which the Sunday school is a part, and gives direction to all the educational work of the church. It provides for the organization, guidance, and supervision of the church school and of its three divisions: children's, youth, adult. It elects, trains, and counsels with teachers and certain officers of the church school concerning the literature they use, their work, the standards of the school, and other matters.

This Commission has many other specific duties, especially concerning the great responsibility of the church school. The General Board of Education is the general agency of the church corresponding to this Commission. The Division of Local Church of this Board has many helps for church school workers and for this Commission.

3. **The Commission on Missions** is the local church auxiliary to the General Board of Missions. It cooperates with the pastor, the Woman's Society, the church school, and other church organizations in the development of the missionary life and spirit in the local church, especially in fourth Sunday programs and offerings for missions and World Service, and in the support of missionary "specials" by individuals, organizations, and the whole church. It provides for the diffusion of missionary information and the distribution of missionary literature and materials. In cooperation with others in the local church, it provides each year for a church-wide school of missions, and, among other things, it studies the community and adjacent areas with reference to the need of missionary projects being sponsored by the local church.

4. **The Commission on Stewardship and Finance** is the group that enables the other commissions and the whole church to operate adequately. Under the authority and direction of the Official Board, this Commission promotes and administers the financial program of the church (¶¶ 261-272). When the annual budget has been approved by the Official Board, this Commission,

under the direction of the board, shall proceed to assure an income sufficient to cover this budget, and shall administer the funds received according to the plan outlined in the *Discipline* (¶ 267) with whatever modifications are deemed best by the board.

5. **The Commission on Christian Social Concerns** was made a required commission by the 1960 General Conference. "The commission shall develop and promote programs and study and action projects in the following areas of Christian social concern: temperance, health, and welfare; peace and world order; and human relations and economics affairs. To this end, it may divide its membership into three sub-committees of approximately equal size, patterned after the divisions of the general board." (¶ 274.3)

Church Committees

For the promoting of other interests and activities in the local church, the Official Board shall create from its own membership and from the membership of the church such committees as it may judge necessary, taking care that these committees do not overlap or conflict with the Quarterly Conference committees. It is required that one member of each committee be a member of the Official Board, so that the board may have a direct personnel contact with each committee. Each of these committees is responsible to the board and reports to the board. The following are some of the possible committees: nominations, music, parsonage, church property, good literature, hospitals and homes, and men's work.

Woman's Society of Christian Service

Every Methodist church is required to have a Woman's Society of Christian Service whose purpose is "to unite all the women of the church in Christian living and service; to help develop and support Christian work among women and children around the world; to develop the spiritual life; to study the needs of the world; to take part in such service activities as will strengthen the local church and improve civic, community, and world conditions" (*Discipline,* ¶¶ 281,282). The women of the church do an untold amount of good, both locally and worldwide, through this organization.

The Church Conference

The affairs of the local church are brought yet closer to the membership by a provision for a Church Conference composed of members of the church who are eighteen years of age or over. The Pastor or Quarterly Conference or District Superintendent may call the Conference. The Church Conference may review the work of the church and adopt plans for further work. See paragraphs 196 and 197 in the *Discipline* for the distinction between a Church Conference and an Annual Church Conference authorized by the Quarterly Conference.

The Pastor

In THE METHODIST CHURCH the Pastor is given a place of responsibility, dignity, and authority. He is appointed (not called) by the Bishop or District Superintendent. He is "in charge of a Station or Circuit." (A Station is one church. A Circuit is more than one church in charge of a Pastor.)

The duties of a Pastor are set forth in 28 brief paragraphs in the *Discipline.* Important in this list of duties are the following: 1. To preach the gospel. 2. To perform the marriage ceremony. 3. To administer the sacraments of Baptism and the Lord's Supper. 4. To visit from house to house. 5. To control the appointment of all services held in his church or churches, in the absence of the District Superintendent or Bishop. 6. To instruct candidates for membership in our doctrines, rules, and regulations. 7. To receive persons into membership. 8. To promote the various interests of the Church, such as: evangelism, Christian education, Christian stewardship, missions and benevolent giving, temperance, Bible reading, and the circulation of Christian literature. 9. To form classes of the children, youth, and adults.

51

All Pastors are appointed to their charges for one year, but may be re-assigned to the same charge year after year for as long a time as the Bishop and Cabinet may deem wise.

The District Superintendent

The office of District Superintendent (formerly called Presiding Elder) is a distinct feature of the polity of Methodism. The District Superintendent is appointed by the Bishop from among the traveling elders of the Annual Conference to supervise the work within a given district. Districts vary in size from about twenty pastoral charges in sparsely-settled areas to sixty or more in cosmopolitan centers. Like the pastor, the District Superintendent receives his appointment for one year, but may be re-assigned for a maximum of six successive years.

The duties of a District Superintendent are many and varied. Among them are these: 1. To travel and preach throughout the district; 2. To supervise the spiritual and temporal affairs of the Church in his district; 3. To preside at Quarterly and District Conferences; and 4. To represent the pastors and churches of his district in the Bishop's cabinet in planning the work of the Conference and in making the appointments.

The Bishop

In THE METHODIST CHURCH the Bishops are elected by the Jurisdictional Conferences, or Central Conferences. The tenure of office is for life, except in the case of Central Conferences as stated above.

Some of the major duties of a Bishop, as set out in the *Discipline* are: 1. To travel throughout the Connection; 2. To oversee the spiritual and temporal affairs of the Church; 3. To appoint preachers to their charges after consultation with the District Superintendents; 4. To preside at Annual, Central, Jurisdictional, and General Conferences; and 5. To attend the meetings of the Council of Bishops of the Church at large, and the College of Bishops of his own Jurisdiction, and to assist in planning the general program and policy of the Church.

CHAPTER IV

METHODIST FIELDS OF SERVICE

THE METHODIST CHURCH may be said to represent the *trained mind,* the *warm heart,* and the *serving hand.* John Wesley was taught at his mother's knee for the first eleven years of his life. The next five years he was a student in Charterhouse School, London. Thereafter he attended Oxford University where he received the degree of Master of Arts.

Then followed his heart-warming experience at the Aldersgate Street prayer meeting. Three symbols, therefore, may be said to represent Methodism: a lighted lamp, a burning altar, and a serving hand; or education, spirituality, and service. Out from his heart-warming experience he went forth *to serve.*

We are now to see in a limited way what the Methodism which he founded is doing in the world.

I

Education

From the time Wesley founded Kingswood School near Bristol, England, to the present time, THE METHODIST CHURCH has had an educational program. It has founded and supported hundreds of schools, colleges and universities. Some of these did not live long, but many which had even a brief existence have justified the time, labor and money invested in them.

THE METHODIST CHURCH has 123 separate chartered universities and colleges connected with The Division of Educational Institutions of the Board of Education. These have more than 201,000 students and 10,065 faculty members. Their buildings and endowments are valued at about $1,010,100,000.00. There are 469 units of the Methodist Student Movement, of which 181 are Wesley Foundations. There are 12 seminaries in which more than 3,500 young ministers are training.

In addition to these educational institutions in the home field, there are others widely distributed in the mission fields. In the mountain sections there are schools for white and colored. There are schools for Mexican and Indian young people. In fact our evangelistic program does not proceed far either at home or abroad until we face the need of a trained leadership in all branches of our work—medicine, agriculture, science, law, education and religion. Without our schools, colleges, and universities our success would be greatly limited.

It has been said repeatedly that there is no such thing as Christian mathematics, history, or science. However, the atmosphere in which these subjects are taught should be one of reverence and faith rather than of cynicism and doubt. A fine statement by a committee of the General Board of Education is in part as follows: "Without apology, the Methodist institution must seek to win its students to the Christ. Our schools must be Christian without apology and Methodist with pride. Our faculties must be Christian in fact. Our efforts must be to make the students Christian just as truly as we try to teach them to think. We must seek to graduate Christians as certainly as we graduate doctors, lawyers, musicians."

The Local Church School

Every Methodist church must have a church school for the purpose of "discharging the church's responsibility for instructing and guiding its entire constituency in Christian faith and living." The church school, in which the Sunday school is the largest organization, shall provide for "education in the Holy Scriptures, the Christian religion, and the Christian Church (leading to commitment to Christ and to church membership) through worship, fellowship, study, and service." (*Discipline,* ¶ 241.)

In 1963 there were 37,372 Church Schools in the congregations of THE METHODIST CHURCH with 6,837,464 members, and an average attendance of 3,685,049 at Sunday School and 610,355 at Sunday Evening Fellowship activities. There were 1,521,719 enrolled in Daily Vacation Church Schools.

Each week a vast number of pieces of literature are being circulated in the departments and classes of these schools. This literature deals with the lessons from the Bible, the doctrines of the Church and the problems that face youth, adults, and the home. Able writers discuss social conditions and all manner of questions that arise in our complex civilization. No Church surpasses ours in its literature and few Churches have reached our high standard of excellence and adaptability to the needs of these millions of people in country, village and city. It is estimated that 6,807,080 pieces of church school literature are distributed each quarter. This adds up to more than 27,000,000 pieces yearly. This great volume of wholesome reading matter is as good seed scattered abroad. Its influence in forming high ideals and molding Christian character cannot be overstated.

The *Discipline* provides for the organization of the Children's Division, the Youth Division and the Adult Division in each Church School.

II

Missions

From the days of John Wesley and Charles Wesley, who were both in a real sense missionaries to Georgia, and of Thomas Coke, who died at sea en route to the mission field, our great Methodist movement has been evangelistic and missionary in spirit. The command of our divine Lord to go into all the world and preach the gospel has been taken in serious and prayerful obedience. Today the vast extent of our missions reaches around the globe.

Mission Fields

Our mission work in the United States includes both the continent and the outlying territory such as Alaska, Hawaii, Puerto Rico, and the Dominican Republic. We have missions in Burma, China, India, Pakistan, Japan, Korea, the Philippines, Africa, Malaya, Sumatra, Europe, and Latin America.

1. CHINA

For many years, China was one of the largest American Methodist mission fields, but in recent years has been in the hands of the Communists. In the vast lands of China and Manchuria there live more than 650,000,000 people—one-fourth of the world's population—more people than there are on the continents of North America, South America, and Africa combined.

Beginning with Robert Morrison, in 1807, modern Christian missions made a vital impact on that great nation. American Methodists began work in China in 1847. After a slow start the work grew rapidly. At the centennial celebration in Foochow in 1947, one of the national Chinese Methodist bishops baptized a little girl who was of the sixth generation of Christians in Foochow and a direct descendant of one of Methodism's first converts in China.

It so happens, however, that 1947 is the last year for which we have statistical information for Methodism on the mainland of China. During that year the ten Annual Conferences reported a total of 91,304 full members, 27,015 preparatory members, and 1,088 local and ordained ministers. Soon after that the more than 200 missionaries had to leave the field, and the Chinese Methodists had to assume full charge. Most of the missionaries went to other fields of mission labor: Taiwan, Sarawak, Sumatra, Burma, Malaya, and Singapore, and the teeming city of Hong Kong, so close to the Mainland.

The Christians on the Mainland have worked under severe handicaps. Probably many of them suffered hardships and persecutions not unlike the early days of Christianity. We know little of what has been happening, but we do know that the churches are alive. We know that the Mid-China and the East China Conferences met in 1956. Since then there has been a turn for the worse. Although the Chinese Christians have suffered terribly during the last four years, we know that some of the churches do remain. The Church lives, and will live.

2. INDIA

Change, too, has been going on in India. Today she is a free nation, one of the most populous on earth, and promises to become great in the family of nations.

We must abandon many of our old ideas about this nation of more than 400,000,000 people whose density of population is 200 per square mile. For centuries poverty, illiteracy, and disease, resulting from many backward circumstances, have held India down. But in recent years she has adopted a democratic constitution, has legally banned untouchability, undertaken land reclamation, and is making plans for industrial and scientific development. Her top leaders have been liberal minded and competent. The whole country has manifested a spirit of self-reliance and faces the future with much hope.

About 100 years ago, in January, 1856, our Methodist Mission in India was opened by the Rev. William Butler and his wife. They were appointed by Bishop Matthew Simpson. In 1864 the India Mission Conference was organized. Today there are ten Annual Conferences which report a total of 158,159 full members and 298,804 preparatory members.

Recent years have witnessed a revolution in the social and economic life of India. In the wake of political independence there have been far-reaching changes in the entire national structure, and it is imperative that the American people seek to have a sympathetic understanding of India today.

India has placed restrictions on missionaries which will affect both their work and the number admitted to that country. Though voices can be heard to the contrary, missionaries are still wanted in India. The new policy of the Government emphasizes the need for the best Christian experience as well as vocational and professional training, but the request for new missionaries to help India must now come from the Churches of India herself through her National Christian Council.

Many new churches and parsonages have been built, and the Indians themselves have given increased financial support.

3. PAKISTAN

Pakistan, one of the newest members of the family of nations, has the same birthday as India, August 15, 1947. There are about 400,000 Christians in this country. All of the 39,000 Methodists are in West Pakistan. The work is carried on in three districts, which are still related to our work in India.

There has been religious freedom in this Mohammedan country up to the present time, and the churches have been able to work without hindrance. Nevertheless, the Christians have a distinct minority feeling, and our Methodist missions must be greatly strengthened there.

4. AFRICA

The total population of Africa, the second largest of the continents, is probably not more than 200,000,000. The Negroes are by far the most numerous of the many races of Africa.

Regarded for centuries as "The Dark Continent," Africa's civilization has been at low ebb over most of the continent. While cannibalism still exists to some extent, while slavery is practiced, and while polygamy is widespread, there is a high state of civilization in many sections, especially in South Africa.

"Nobody knows how many tongues are actually used, but nearly 850 different languages and dialects have already been listed. Many of these have not yet been reduced to writing." For years Frank Laubach has been teaching backward tribes to read and write and has been a great blessing to Africa and Christian missions.

Methodist missionary work in Africa is being carried on in Algeria, Tunisia, Liberia, Angola, Belgian Congo, Southern Rhodesia, Mozambique, Portuguese East Africa, and in the Transvaal.

In spite of the political and racial tensions that have gripped a large part of Africa in recent years, the Church in Africa has developed remarkably in its physical property. The Board of Missions reports: "Many new churches have been built, new schools have come into being, hospitals have been erected, shops and agricultural equipment have been provided, so that the missionaries and nationals, as never before, have tools at their disposal to carry on their assignments." Much of this new equipment has come from African resources.

In Christian stewardship, the African Church is becoming more mature. The African leaders feel the responsibility of propagating the faith and are aware that the hope of the continent is in the Church of Jesus Christ.

Another encouraging development in the Church in Africa has been the gradual transfer of leadership from missionary to African personnel. In the midst of the present upheaval (1960) the African Christians testify that they still need the missionaries and want them to remain. There is so much to do.

5. JAPAN

Now that the period of post-war occupation of Japan is over, there has been steady progress in Christian thought and action among the Japanese people. Japan is still debating democracy as a national policy and Christianity as a source of moral and spiritual vigor.

The United "Church of Christ" is the main Protestant contender for Japanese loyalties, and THE METHODIST CHURCH is the largest of the eight denominations which merged their mission work in Japan in this Church of Christ in Japan (Nihon Kirisuto Kyodan). Our Board of Missions operates in Japan through a joint committee made up of the several cooperating denominations. This is a great forward step.

Though we Methodists have 150 missionaries in Japan, the need is not yet fully met. Japan is the potential leader of all Asia, and there must be no relaxation of our concern that Japan be a Christian nation.

In the midst of post-war confusion the Japanese Church turned its attention directly to evangelistic effort. Nationwide revivals were initiated under the leadership of Toyohiko Kagawa and American evangelists, with outstanding results. Tens of thousands of decisions were made for the Christian way of life.

Great strides were also made in visitation and personal evangelism, with large numbers of laymen taking part.

Since almost every home in Japan has a radio, and almost every adult can read, the Japanese are approachable through Christian broadcasting, literature, and newspaper evangelism, and other media of mass education and evangelism. It is both significant and encouraging that there are now 260,000 students enrolled in Christian schools in Japan.

6. KOREA

For decades, Korea was one of the most fertile Christian mission fields, and the work of Methodist missions abounded there. Then came World War II, its resultant division of Korea into two parts, and, finally, the communist invasion of 1950 from the north which disrupted the Christian movement and turned all of South Korea (Republic of Korea) into a land ravaged by war and filled with carnage, destruction, and suffering.

In the wake of the holocaust, on November 3, 1951, a special session of the General Conference of the Korean Methodist Church was held. A native Korean was elected as Bishop; new plans were made for Annual Conferences and for the reorganization of local churches.

Christians now hold leadership in this land out of all proportion to their numbers. The Korean Methodist constituency has increased from 40,000 to almost 125,000 persons. There are 1,095 Methodist churches and chapels and 1,011 Sunday schools. There are already about 90 missionaries and about 1,200 ordained and supply pastors in 25 Districts and three Annual Conferences. Korea is so receptive to the gospel that our missionary forces need to be doubled even yet. Korea seems "ripe for the harvest." Let us pray that "the Lord of the harvest" will send laborers; let us give of our sons and daughters and of our resources.

7. THE PHILIPPINES

Immediately after the Spanish-American War, Bishop James Thoburn preached in Manila and Methodism entered the Philippines. The growth of our work there has resulted in 495 organized churches and 898 regular preaching places with 73,159 full members and 57,671 preparatory members.

During recent years more than 100 Methodist churches were built, rebuilt, or repaired, and a comparable number of parsonages and other buildings. In a nation that is mostly rural, Philippine Methodism is giving its attention to rural problems and to the people who live in small cities, towns, and "barrios." A score of churches and work centers have been opened in Mindanao and other nearby islands.

The Philippine Church is strongly evangelistic. Its vitality is shown in its rapid expansion, its self-support, and its dedicated young people who have gone out as missionaries.

8. SOUTHEAST ASIA

Thriving mission work was being carried on in this section of the globe before World War II. The work was reopened following liberation and now goes on with renewed enthusiasm.

Sarawak, the "Land of Decision" of the 1956-60 quadrennium, has seen the greatest growth of the church of any land in this area. As Ibans have come seeking baptism, a whole new missionary force has been recruited to minister to them. Christian nurses and doctors, preachers and teachers have come from many lands.

In Burma there was much political unrest until new leadership took over in 1958. Mission work has been under terrific handicaps. Nevertheless congregations and schools have served well and Methodist membership has doubled since the war.

In Malaya the missionary ranks have been considerably strengthened by missionaries who were forced to leave China because of Communist pressure. In August 1957 Malaya became an independent nation. Never have the Malayan leaders been more cordial and more openly appreciative of what the church has done. Within the Chinese churches in Malaya there is a growing spirit to evangelize.

Singapore elected its first independent government in 1959

and the Methodist schools and churches are now growing both in number and influence.

9. EUROPE

There are Methodist Conferences in the following nations of Europe: Belgium, Austria, Czechoslovakia, Denmark, Finland and Sweden, Norway, Germany, Switzerland, and Hungary. Methodism is also at work in Yugoslavia, Bulgaria, Poland, Scandinavia, and Italy, although under very difficult circumstances in many cases. During recent years the Church in Germany has grown steadily, and more than one half of the churches destroyed during the war have already been rebuilt. In 1963 the Methodist Conferences in Europe reported a total of 117,021 full members and 18,133 preparatory members.

10. LATIN AMERICA

Our Church is at work in 10 Latin American countries: Mexico, Cuba, Costa Rica, Panama, Peru, Chile, Bolivia, Uruguay, Argentina, and Brazil. These countries comprise a very needy and most promising mission field for Protestant Christianity. The last several years have been years of real advance and development of the Church in many of these countries. The membership of the Protestant churches has been increasing more rapidly than the population.

Funds from the Week of Dedication, the Crusade, and the Advance have aided greatly in the building of churches in these Latin American countries. More than 100 new church buildings were constructed during a single quadrennium. A number of them were built entirely with funds raised on the field.

For some years now the three Divisions of the Board of Missions (World Missions, National Missions, and the Woman's Division) have requested the cooperation of the General Board of Evangelism in sponsoring evangelistic missions in other countries. Such missions have been held in every Latin American country named above, in Hawaii, Alaska, India, Korea, and in the Philippines. These missions accomplish much good. If only every Methodist could visit the mission fields for himself, how much good would be accomplished!

A World Parish

"The foreign work of THE METHODIST CHURCH is a church within the church—larger than many American denominations." It embraces:

45 nations—125 languages
1,555 missionaries and 4,060 ordained national ministers
9,000 churches and preaching places (estimated)
1,584,128 full and preparatory members
878 schools and colleges
118 medical centers
112 social service institutions

The Board of Missions extends the Church and is the greatest educational force of Methodism. It maintains more educational institutions than all the other agencies combined. In foreign countries it operates 878 schools—including 16 junior colleges, 21 senior colleges and universities, 3 medical schools, 27 theological seminaries, 12 teachers colleges, 21 nurses training schools, 21 Bible schools, 260 high schools, and about 500 elementary schools.

The Board of Missions in its great work operates more hospitals and medical dispensaries than all other Methodist agencies combined. There are more such Methodist institutions in foreign fields than in America. Many of these hospitals and clinics are among people who have no other access to modern medical science and who have recourse only to medicine men and witch doctors. These number 38 hospitals, 80 clinics and dispensaries, 3 medical schools, 21 nurses training schools, and 8 leprosariums.

The Board assists in the support of over 2,600 pastors and workers in Home Mission fields in the United States. It maintains 26 colleges and schools, 10 hospitals, 97 urban centers, 32 larger parishes, 3 mountain missions, 69 homes, orphanages and dormitories, 119 Goodwill Industries, 141 churches of American Indians, 33 homes for old people, 12 deaconess homes, 24 Esther Halls or hostels, 4 friendship Homes for Negro girls.

In Puerto Rico, Santo Domingo, Alaska, and Hawaii it supports 185 workers and pastors, 3 hospitals, and 4 orphanages.

Its evangelistic ministry includes more than 500 churches among Orientals, Latin Americans, American Indians in continental United States, and in Alaska, Hawaii, and Puerto Rico. It assists with the support of nearly 2,000 evangelistic workers—Negro ministers, foreign-speaking pastors, deaconesses, and missionary pastors in rural and industrial areas.

Its building ministry helps Methodist congregations throughout the country to secure adequate sanctuaries. At present the Church Extension section has loans out to more than 1,200 churches. It helps many churches and parsonages in new and struggling situations with donations which usually total over one million dollars annually, and it provides architectural service, debt-raising service, and fund-raising service to scores of congregations. It provides counsel in social and industrial relations and in research and surveys, training conferences for pastors, and field administration. It cooperates with all interdenominational bodies in related fields.

Truly, the work of the Board is both total and global!

Woman's Division of Christian Service

In the Woman's Division of Christian Service which is a part of the Board of Missions there are 30,514 local organizations of the Woman's Society of Christian Service with a total membership of 1,718,986.

During the average year the local societies send about $12,000,000 to their conference treasurers, besides raising and spending an additional total of about $18,000,000 for work in their local communities.

The above gifts make possible the support of scores of institutions, as well as approximately 1,250 missionaries and deaconesses, about equally divided between home and foreign lands. These render a wide variety of Christian service in many areas of the United States and its dependencies, as well as in Burma, India, Malaya, Sumatra, China, all sections of Africa, Japan, Korea, the Philippine Islands, Latin America, and Europe. They are at work in schools and colleges, children's homes, social centers, hospitals and clinics, rural and urban projects, all part of a great program of Kingdom building. Assisting them is found approximately 4,000 trained nationals attached to missions staffs on foreign fields.

Undergirding all of this is a program of education carried forward through the local societies in their regular meetings and through hundreds of study classes on current topics related to trends in missions, spiritual life needs, and social action. Leadership training is a major emphasis in Jurisdiction and Conference schools and institutes, preparing annually a host of women for more effective Christian service.

The Board of Publication

According to legend Martin Luther once threw his ink bottle at the devil, but John Wesley hurled an entire printing press at him! Francis Asbury wisely said that the religious press "is next in importance to the preaching of the gospel."

Two weeks before George Washington became President of the United States (April 30, 1789) twenty-five Methodist preachers met in John Street Chapel, New York City, and founded The Methodist Publishing House. "The tradition of Methodist publishing is older still. John Wesley was the father of it. . . . He really started the Methodist book business. He trained his preachers to sell books and taught both preachers and people to read books. . . . It should never be forgotten by Methodists that their founder was the most prolific author and publisher of his time, and that he earned and gave away $150,000.00 by it."

In America John Dickins was the first Publishing Agent. The progress of this enterprise is indicated by the following quotations from *The Story of The Methodist Publishing House:*

65

"At the time of Unification, the publishing interests of the Church consisted of two corporations of The Methodist Episcopal Church with houses in New York, Cincinnati, Chicago, Boston, Pittsburgh, Detroit, Kansas City, San Francisco, and Portland, Ore.; one corporation of the Methodist Episcopal Church, South, with houses in Nashville, Dallas, and Richmond; and one corporation of the Methodist Protestant Church, with houses in Baltimore and Pittsburgh. The corporations were preserved under the new Board of Publication and the thirteen houses set strategically from coast to coast" have been maintained. "More than a million books are printed and bound in these plants every year. Approximately a hundred million copies of periodicals pour from their presses every year, and carry their Methodist messages all over the world." From the beginning some of the proceeds of The Publishing House have been used to help support superannuated ministers and their dependents. For 1963, for example, the appropriation to Conference Claimants is $600,000.00. This brings the total distributed since the founding of The Publishing House to $20,865,000.00.

This is a magnificent record of conscientious and successful management. In recent years Cokesbury Book Stores have been opened in Atlanta, Boston, and Los Angeles.

Christian Social Concerns

At the 1960 General Conference the Board of Christian Social Concerns was created. Its purpose was defined as: "To lift up before the members of the church and also the secular world the Christian concern for personal, social, and civic righteousness, to analyze the issues which confront the nation and the world as well as the local community and the person, and to propose Christian lines of action."

Since this new board replaced three former boards (Temperance, World Peace, and Social and Economic Relations), it operates under three divisions. They are: The Division of Temperance and General Welfare; the Division of Peace and World

Order; and the Division of Human Relations and Economic Affairs.

The regular members of the new board are assigned to one of these divisions. The Board of Social Concerns has one general secretary and three associate general secretaries. "Each of the associate general secretaries shall have primary responsibility for those Christian social concerns which are assigned to his particular division. Within this area and under the direction of the division and its executive committee, he with his staff shall develop a program of research, education, and action, bringing these concerns to the attention of the denomination and all its churches and of the communities they serve." (¶ 1531.2)

The headquarters of the general board and of its divisions is in Washington, D. C. In addition to the general headquarters there is a New York United Nations office conducted in co-operation with the Woman's Division of Christian Service of the Board of Missions. The Division of Peace and World Order represents the board in this office.

Lay Activities

The growing place of leadership and usefulness of laymen in THE METHODIST CHURCH has resulted in the organization of the Board of Lay Activities. The purpose of this Board is "to deepen the spiritual life of the lay members of the church and cultivate in them an increasing loyalty and interest that they may become an active working force in each local church."

The Board, with headquarters in Evanston, has an extensive program which includes Christian stewardship; Christian fellowship; personal evangelism; lay speaking; adequate support of the ministry; sound church finance; attendance upon worship; training of Official Boards; and other items.

In the local church provision is made for the lay leader to cooperate with the pastor; and also for the organization of Methodist Men. The objectives of this organization are five, in brief as follows:

1. To seek Christ's way of life.

2. To learn more about The Methodist Church.
3. To endeavor to win men and boys to Christ and the Church.
4. To promote Christian fellowship in the Church.
5. To cooperate in promoting the total program of the Church.

Hospitals and Homes

The Church carries on a ministry to the sick, the aged, the homeless children, and other needy persons because of the desire to carry out the ministry of her Lord and to meet great needs.

Methodism's interest in Christian philanthropy goes back to 1740 when George Whitefield made a decision which brought about the Bethesda Orphanage of Savannah, Georgia.

Now the Board of Hospitals and Homes, with offices in Evanston, has an advisory relationship to every hospital and home which is owned or supervised by any agency of The Methodist Church in the United States. In this capacity, it has 236 affiliated institutions. Seventy-six of these are hospitals, 104 are homes for older persons, 49 are child care agencies, and 7 are homes for business women. These institutions have a total of 35,135 full-time employees and served 1,520,913 persons in 1959. Nearly all of the hospitals operate schools of nursing, and in them 6,482 nurses were in training in January, 1959. A total of $14,428,751 free service was rendered by the institutions in 1959, including that made possible in the hospitals by the Golden Cross Society (¶ 1559, *Discipline*). The 49 Methodist Child Care Agencies and Homes for children annually serve 6,600 "little ones," providing either group care, foster homes, or adoption services.

The aim of the philanthropic institutions of the Church is to live up to the highest scientific standards of service and also to add a plus element—the Christian influence. They follow Jesus who "went about doing good" and "healing all manner of sickness." They remember that He said, "He who believes in me will also do the works that I do; and greater works than these shall he do."

Television, Radio, and Film Commission

The 1952 General Conference established a Radio and Film Commission, and in 1956 its name was enlarged to include television. Its purpose and function, among other things, are to "unify and co-ordinate the audio-visual programs of all Methodist agencies dealing with projected pictures, recordings, transcriptions, radio and television programs, and other audio-visual materials." It makes studies in the audio-visual field and produces and distributes such programs and materials. With headquarters at Nashville, Tennessee, this Commission is now well staffed and has already produced some notable materials.

News and Information

THE METHODIST CHURCH maintains a Commission on Public Relations and Methodist Information which has offices in New York, Evanston, Washington, and Nashville, and official representatives in several other cities. This Commission gathers news of public interest concerning Methodist activities and opinion and disseminates it through the secular press, the religious press, radio, and television.

Evangelism

One of the most useful of these great Boards is the General Board of Evangelism. This Board, responsible for developing and promoting the evangelistic spirit in the Church, promotes all forms of evangelism that by all means and methods persons may be won for Christ and that church members may be built up in spiritual life and faith. To this Board is entrusted also the great responsibility of promoting the practice of prayer and of individual and family worship, as well as stimulating the entire membership of the Church in worship and in Christian service.

For its work this Board is divided into various departments, such as Evangelists, Area and Conference Evangelism, District Evangelism, Local Church Evangelism, Preaching Evangelism, the Cooperative Department of Youth Evangelism, the Tidings Department for the publishing of non-denominational evangelistic literature, Methodist Evangelistic Materials for strictly Methodist materials, and The Upper Room Department which has blessed the world with its devotional materials.

Methodists ought to be "method-ists" in their devotional life. Every home and every church member should have daily devotions; and the bi-monthly periodical, *The Upper Room,* is unsurpassed in its ministry in building up the devotional life. It is the most widely read devotional booklet and religious periodical in the world. Truly, its circulation of 3,500,000 copies of each English issue is phenomenal. It is printed in 38 foreign language editions and the Braille English and "Talking Book" editions also.

For several years this Board made much progress in promoting great campaigns of pulpit, visitation, and spiritual life evangelism in metropolitan areas, in Districts, in Annual Conferences, and in Episcopal Areas. While these united and simultaneous efforts continue, wherever the local leadership requests them, each church is urged "to seek and to save" persons as its constant purpose and effort the year around.

Recently the Department of Local Church Evangelism has been enlarged in order that it might serve the local church more adequately. The divisions of the Department coincide closely with the disciplinary duties of the Local Church Commission on Membership and Evangelism. This Department is concerned with these facets of evangelism: Prospect Discovery and Cultivation, Personal Evangelism, Visitation Evangelism, Church Attendance, Membership Care and Conservation, Prayer and Family Devotions, and Membership Re-establishment.

Promotion and Cultivation

"In order to co-ordinate the promotion of the general benevolence causes of The Methodist Church, to the end that our people may be informed about, and may adequately support, the work of the general agencies, there shall be a Commission on Promotion and Cultivation." The Commission publishes "The Methodist Story," the program journal for the local church.

Through its central promotional office in Chicago, this Commission promotes throughout the church the program of World Service, Advance Specials for missionary causes and projects, Week of Dedication offerings, and other general financial causes.

Because of the inseparable relationship between education in stewardship and giving, the General Conference has called upon this Commission to cooperate with the Boards of Education and of Lay Activities in a church-wide emphasis upon the stewardship of possessions, which emphasis shall be closely related to World Service and benevolent giving.

The General Conference specified that stewardship of possessions "shall be interpreted to mean that the tithe is the minimum standard of giving for Methodist people" and that Methodist people are to be enlisted as tithers. (¶ 753.4, *Discipline*.)

A Methodist Gives

THE METHODIST CHURCH is a connectional Church with a world program. When a Methodist contributes to the World Service Fund or the general benevolent program of his church, his contribution is divided according to a carefully worked out schedule, and is channeled to many worth-while projects that promote the Kingdom and literally cover the world. In no other way can he make his money go as far and do as much good as in giving to the "World Service" through his own local church.

The "World Service" money paid into a local church treasury is sent by the local church to the Annual Conference treasurer who in turn sends it to the General Treasurer of THE METHODIST CHURCH. This general treasurer, who is the executive secretary of the Council on World Service and Finance, divides the money according to the ratio carefully worked out by the General Conference.

So it is, that when a Methodist gives to World Service he gives a part of himself to Methodist missions at home and abroad; he contributes to Christian education in colleges and universities; invests in Christian education for children, youth, and adults at home and abroad; shares in training ministers for the Church; makes an effort to secure a sober nation; takes part in the protection of homeless youth and the aged; helps support the retired servants of the Church; assists in the program of lay activities; participates in world-wide evangelism; aids in the distribution of the Bible; and votes for a peaceful world. In no other way can he make his money go as far and do as much as in giving to World Service through his own local church.

SUGGESTED BOOKS ON METHODISM

The Methodist Primer, revised edition .50
The Methodist First Reader, Selecman and Jones .50
The Beliefs of a Methodist Christian, Clinton M. Cherry .50
John Wesley, Evangelist, F. Gerald Ensley .50
Primer of Beliefs for Methodist Laymen, Copeland .50
Marks of a Methodist, Kennedy .50
Spiritual Renewal for Methodism, Emerick .50
Pocket Book of Methodist Beliefs, Hazzard .50
Articles of Religion of Methodist Church, Chilcote .50
World Methodist Conference Speaks to World, Nall .50
*The above are available from The Methodist Publishing House
or from Methodist Evangelistic Materials*

LEAFLETS ON METHODISM—$4.00 PER 100

A Heart Strangely Warmed, by H. Cecil Pawson .05
What Methodists Believe, by the Bishops (leaflet) .05
Some Essential Methodist Beliefs, Robert G. Tuttle .05
When Methodists Baptize, F. Gerald Ensley .05
When Methodists Commune, Charles S. Jarvis .05
The Character of a Methodist, by John Wesley .05
I'm Proud to Be a Methodist, Everett W. Palmer .05
Susanna Wesley, Frederick E. Maser .05
The Methodist Church, James S. Chubb ($2.00 per 100)
The General Rules of Methodism ($2.00 per 100)
Five Methodist Beliefs, Bishop Kennedy ($2.00 per 100)
Order from METHODIST EVANGELISTIC MATERIALS,
1908 Grand Avenue, Nashville 5, Tenn.

CHAPTER V

CHURCH MEMBERSHIP

Only one condition was required of those who desired admission to the early Methodist societies: "a desire to flee from the wrath to come and to be saved from their sins." In the present-day language we would probably say: "a sincere desire to be true followers of Jesus Christ and to be saved from their sins."

The *first* step therefore in becoming a member of THE METHODIST CHURCH is a definite commitment of one's life to Christ in repentance, faith, and obedience.

The *second step* is Christian Baptism. Those desiring "to receive holy Baptism" are required "to accept the obligations of this holy Sacrament," by answering certain questions. The Ritual in our *Discipline* contains three forms of baptismal questions: one for infants, in which case the parents take the vow and the person baptized in infancy retakes it when joining the church in later years; one for children and youth; and one for adults.

The Baptism of Infants

Then shall the Minister address the Parents or Sponsors, as follows: "Dearly beloved, forasmuch as *this child is* now presented by you for Christian Baptism, and *is* thus consecrated to God and to his Church, it is your part and duty to see that *he* be taught, as soon as *he* shall be able to learn, the meaning and purpose of this holy Sacrament; that *he* be instructed in the principles of our holy faith and the nature of the Christian life; that *he* shall be trained to give reverent attendance upon the public and private worship of God and the teaching of the Holy Scripture, and that in every way, by precept and example, you shall seek to lead *him* into the love of God and the service of our Lord Jesus Christ.

"Do you solemnly promise to fulfill these duties so far as in you lies, the Lord being your helper?
"We do."

The Baptism of Children and Youth

"Will you faithfully put away from you every known sin, of thought, word, or deed, and accept and confess Jesus Christ as your Saviour and Lord?
"God helping me, I will.

"Will you diligently study the Bible as God's Holy Word, and in all things strive to make it the rule of your life?
"God helping me, I will.

"Having been taught how the Spirit of our Lord separates right from wrong, will you faithfully endeavor to live so as to be pleasing unto Him?
"God helping me, I will.

"Will you be baptized in this faith?
"This is my desire."

The Baptism of Adults

"Do you truly repent of your sins and accept and confess Jesus Christ as your Saviour and Lord?
"I do.

"Will you earnestly endeavor to keep God's holy will and commandments?
"I will.

"Do you desire to be baptized in this faith?
"I do."

Upon receiving satisfactory answers to these three questions, after a brief prayer the minister shall baptize each person saying, *"N.* (name), I baptize thee in the name of the Father and of the Son and of the Holy Spirit. Amen."

The third and final step in becoming a member of The Methodist Church is by answering certain questions:

Receiving Persons into the Church

The service of receiving persons into the Church opens with a statement to the congregation which begins as follows:

"Dearly beloved, the Church is of God, and will be preserved to the end of time, for the promotion of his worship and the due administration of his word and ordinances, the maintenance of Christian fellowship and discipline, the edification of believers, and the conversion of the world. All, of every age and station, stand in need of the means of grace which it alone supplies. . . ."

Then the minister briefly addresses those who are to be received and asks them to confess their faith by answering the following questions:

Do you here in the presence of God and this congregation renew the solemn promise and vow that was made at your baptism?
I do.

Do you confess Jesus Christ as your Saviour and Lord and pledge your allegiance to his Kingdom?
I do.

Do you receive and profess the Christian faith as contained in the New Testament of our Lord Jesus Christ?
I do.

Will you be loyal to The Methodist Church, and uphold it by your attendance, your prayers, your gifts, and your service?
I will.

Then those to be received shall kneel, and the minister, who may lay his hand upon the head of every one severally, shall say:

N. The Lord defend thee with his heavenly grace and by his Spirit confirm thee in the faith and fellowship of all true disciples of Jesus Christ. Amen.

The minister shall say to the candidates:

We rejoice to recognize you as *members* of the Church of Christ, and bid you welcome to all its privileges; and in token of our brotherly love we give you the right hand of fellowship, and pray that you may be numbered with his people here, and with his saints in glory everlasting.

And the minister shall say to the congregation:

Brethren, I commend to your love and care *these persons* whom we this day recognize as *members* of the Church of Christ. Do all in your power to increase *their* faith, confirm *their* hope, and perfect *them* in love.

75

Receiving Children into the Church

Following a statement to the congregation and a prayer, the minister addresses the parents or sponsors (and sometimes Sunday School teachers) who stand behind the children at the altar:

"Dearly beloved, let this be to you a day of peculiar joy and thanksgiving, in that *these who are* of your flesh and blood have also entered into a holier spiritual kinship with you in Jesus Christ. While the Church will continue to share with you the duty and privileges of bringing up *these children* in the nurture and admonition of the Lord, it renews its solemn injunction to you, by God's help, faithfully to continue both to teach and to train *them,* by example and precept, in the way of the Lord. Will you accept this duty, in the fear and favor of God, and here and now, in the presence of Almighty God and this congregation, renew the vows made by you in the baptism of *these children?*
With God's help, I will.

Then shall the minister address the children who are candidates and say:
Beloved children, our Lord Jesus, by his holy Word, hath expressly given to everyone who believes in him a place in his Kingdom and Church. Before you are admitted into the Church, it becomes my duty to inquire of you as to your purpose of mind and heart:

Do you, *each of you,* believe in God as your heavenly Father?
I do.
Do you accept Jesus Christ as your personal Saviour?
I do.
Do you believe in the Bible as God's holy Word?
I do.
Will you be loyal to The Methodist Church and uphold it by your attendance, your prayers, your gifts, and your service?
I will.

Here the minister may offer an extempore prayer. Then those to be received shall kneel, and the minister, laying his hands upon every one of them severally, shall say:
I receive you into the Church of Christ and pray God to confirm you in the faith and fellowship of all true disciples of Jesus Christ. Amen.

Then shall the minister, the people, and the children pray together the Lord's Prayer.
Our Father who art in heaven, hallowed be thy name; thy kingdom come, thy will be done on earth as it is in heaven. Give us this day our daily bread. And forgive us our trespasses, as we forgive those who trespass against us. And lead us not into temptation, but deliver us from evil. For thine is the kingdom, and the power, and the glory, forever. Amen.

76

INDEX

77